A RAVENOUS FEAST

A RAVENOUS FEAST

Spellbinding Recipes Inspired by the Literary Works of
EDGAR ALLAN POE

Veronica Hinke

weldon**owen**

CONTENTS

FOREWORD BY ART SMITH 7
INTRODUCTION 8

CADAVEROUS APPETIZERS AND PARTY FOODS

Boundaries of Life and Death Party Dip: *Ham Salad* . . 17
C. August Dupin's Charcuterie Board 18
Sinbad the Sailor's Roasted Carrot and Blood-Orange Hummus Boats 21
House of Usher Party Crackers: *Poppy-Seed Crackers with Lemon Thyme* 23
Forest Reverie Butter Board 24
Some Words with a Mummy Appetizer 27
The Pit and the Pendulum Bread: *Gingerbread* 28
Icy Air of Night Fruit Platter 31
Vulture-Eye Deviled Eggs 32
Tavern Biscuits 34
Fortunato's Stuffed Médoc Mushrooms 35
Patatas Bravas 37
Alarum Premature Burial Fruit-Pastry Bites 38
Arthur Gordon Pym's Black-Tree Candy Bark 40
The Poe Toaster's Anchovy Toast Points 41
Roasted Apricots and Bananas Raven Food 42
Tea Cakes 43

BEGUILING SALADS, SIDES, AND SOUPS

Cadaver Rice 47
The Assignation Salad 48
Vanilla-Perfumed Indian Pudding 49
Catacombs Roasted Zucchini and Black Rice with Bell Peppers 50
South Carolina Peaches and Pork Tarantula Pull-Apart Bread 53
Arthur Gordon Pym's Clam Chowder 54
    Oyster Crackers 56

Island of the Fay Rosemary-Scented Baked Stuffed Tomatoes 57
Shattered Mirror Soup: *Pepper-Pot Soup with Meatballs* 59
Chilled Blackberry Médoc Soup with Fresh Mint . . . 60
Annabel Lee's Crab Bisque 63

GHASTLY DELECTABLE MAIN COURSES

Prince Prospero's Roasted Turkey Drumsticks 66
Prince Prospero's Beef Wellington with Port-Wine Duxelles 69
Barbarous Islanders' Lobster Newberg 70
Catacombs Roasted Cauliflower 72
Turkey Pudding with Cherry-Cranberry Compote . . 75
Vulture-Eye Pasta: *Squid Ink Pasta with Pan-Seared Scallops and Raspberry Sauce* 76
Raven's Nests 79
Ghost Pepper Jelly and Cilantro Cream Cheese Tea Sandwiches 80
Descent into the Maelstrom Hashed Cod 81
Raven Black Bean Cakes with Cilantro Crema 82
Vincent Price's Chicken Vermouth with Rice 83

DESOLATELY DELICIOUS DESSERTS

Graveyard Poke Cake 86
Berenice's Teeth: *Cookies and Marshmallow Dessert* 89
The Hideous Heart Dessert 91
Prince Prospero's Uninvited Guest Cake: *Spanish Bun Cake* 92
The City in the Sea Violet Ice Cream 95
    No-Churn Ice Cream 97
William Legrand's Gold-Bug Cake 98
The Cask of Amontillado Dessert Wall 100
Armagnac Brandied Peaches 103

Shadow Cake 105
Ligeia Dream Cake: *Poppy-Seed Cake with Lemon Thyme* 106
Lafourcade Family Graveyard Trifle............ 109
    Tombstone Cookies........................ 110
    Apple Compote 110
    Vanilla Pudding 111
    Mini Chocolate Skulls..................... 111
The Penny Pie Man's Pies 112
    Lemon Pie............................. 112
    Vinegar Pie............................ 113
    Funeral Pie 113
Paradise Pears: *Molasses-Poached Pears with Port Wine*............................ 114
Cask of Amontillado Cannoli 117

Splendorous Sips and Illimitable Mixes

Prince Prospero's Angel of the Odd Kirsch Mulled Wine with Chokeberries.......... 120
Poe Family Eggnog 123
Tintinnabulation Tea Blend 124
The Pit and the Pendulum Spanish Coffee........ 126
The Time Traveler: *Sazerac with Lemon-Thyme Ice* 127
The Oblong Box Cocktail 129
The Sleeper: *Raspberry-Rosemary Shrub Margarita* .. 130
Raspberry-Rosemary Shrub 131
Sangaree 132
Sissy's Syllabub 135
Mr. Monck Mason's Flying Machine Champagne Cocktail...................... 136
Descent into the Maelstrom Punch: *Philadelphia Fish-House Punch*......................... 139
Eureka Punch 140

Apple Hot Punch 141
Blueberry Sherry Cobbler................... 142
William Legrand's Gold-Bug Cocktail.......... 145
The Big-Bang Lavender Water 146
Milk Punch............................. 147

Sagacious Entertaining: Planning the Perfect Gothic-Glam Gathering

Gothic Fetes and Festivals................... 150
    Hideous Hints and Ideas................. 152
Dos and Don'ts of Victorian Entertaining 153
Trialed Trivia Questions.................... 154
Cryptography Game 155
How to Host a Medieval Murder-Mystery Dinner Party............................ 157
How to Play Poe's Favorite Card Games......... 158
Song List 159

Acknowledgments 160
Bibliography 161
Index 162
About the Author..................... 167

FOREWORD

Edgar Allan Poe once said: "If a poem hasn't ripped apart your soul, you haven't experienced poetry." The same can be said for the power of good food and beverage. There is little that can satisfy the soul as much as delicious food that is lovingly prepared, and especially when shared among dear friends, family, and anyone who shares a passion for drinking, dining, and gathering. These aspects are so important to me in every one of my restaurants and in every meal I prepare. Even better is when a menu is grounded in the history of our great nation. In this cooking and entertaining guide, which is dedicated to the life and stories of Poe, one of America's first great authors, Veronica Hinke presents painstaking research that highlights some of the most interesting characteristics of food and drink of the American antebellum period. The era is distinct in the soul of American culinary history. It was many years after the American Revolution, yet the culinary culture of 1840s America, Poe's world, remained steadfastly centered on English comfort foods. There were poultry-laden puddings steamed for hours over flames on wood-burning stoves, hearty tavern biscuits and tea cakes, trifles made of voluptuous layers of indulgent cakes, puddings, and creams. It would be decades before Americans began embracing the French culinary styles that became so popular in the early 20th century. The street food genre that is so prevalent today also stems from this time period and is presented in this book. It is so important that we continue to learn as much as we can about the history of American cuisine and keep that history alive and shared. Like good poetry, the value of good food and drink to our souls is immeasurable. I hope this culinary guide, which intertwines literature and culinary history, will provide the perfect canvas upon which to create meaningful gatherings that celebrate both.

Art Smith
JAMES BEARD AWARD–WINNING CHEF

INTRODUCTION

This collection of recipes is inspired by the literary works of Edgar Allan Poe, and also the time period in which Poe lived and worked. Much of what we know of the era is because of Poe. Steadfast aspects of our popular culture today—including the modern detective mystery—stem from this era, through Poe. What's even more awe-inspiring is how Poe made his profound mark in history during a time when American literature was only just starting to be defined.

In the uncharted waters of 1841, the world met Poe's character C. Auguste Dupin in his short story "The Murders in the Rue Morgue." Dupin was the first character in literature to solve the case at the center of a story. It would take nearly half a century longer for someone, Sir Arthur Conan Doyle, to run with Poe's inspiration with a similarly unforgettable mastermind creation of the beloved character Sherlock Holmes.

From brilliant, beautiful prose and poetry ("The Forest Reverie," "Ligeia") to deeply disturbing and grotesque tales ("The Black Cat," "The Tell-Tale Heart"), Poe's range in literature was exceptional. He was incredibly gifted with words and is credited with inventing hundreds of them. Even more words became mainstream after he daylighted them.

Because much of his work focuses on the macabre—premature, live burials in family cemeteries ("Berenice"), live burials behind catacomb walls ("The Cask of Amontillado")—Poe and his stories are highly celebrated and memorialized on the occasion of Halloween and the surrounding season. Actors engage in reenactment poetry readings in historic houses and museums. People everywhere try to capture the spirit and essence that Poe conveyed.

This book offers ideas and recipes for those who respect the culture Poe created and gifted to us, by creating atmospheric dinner celebrations, parties, and other festive gatherings that evoke Poe's life and works. There are fun seasonal recipes for Raven Food (dried cherries, apricots, and bananas roasted in maple syrup with nuts); a delicious creepy-crawly giant tarantula pull-apart bread; and a luscious coconut cake shimmering in gold polish and shaped like the code-carrying insect in Poe's short story "The Gold-Bug."

Just as importantly, this is also a guide for home cooks of all ages and abilities who want to interpret the era in which Poe lived and worked, through food and drink. From a pudding with cherry-cranberry compote to pears painstakingly poached in port wine and molasses, there are numerous period recipes with modern measurements and ideas for presentation. Armagnac Brandied Peaches represent the brandied fruits that were popular in the Northeastern Seaboard states where Poe lived and worked.

These recipes also highlight significant information that was unearthed in recent years about Poe's diet and that of his wife, Virginia Clemm. Dr. Stephen Macko studied samples of Poe's hair, burning it at 1832° F to convert it to gas. He purified the gases using a gas chromatograph. Measurements of isotopes of carbon, nitrogen, and sulfur revealed that Poe and his wife's diet, although rich in common foods of the era, including beans, potatoes, chicken, beef, and pork, consisted mostly of seafood. Christopher P. Semtner, curator of the Poe Museum in Richmond, Virginia, highlighted the findings of the studies of Poe's hair in an article in the Autumn 2017 issue of *The Edgar Allan Poe Review*. The article is titled "Poe in Richmond: Poe's Tell-Tale Hair at the Poe Museum."

In light of the newly revealed information, there are recipes for lobster Newberg, crab bisque, clam chowder, and other classic New England dishes. These seafood recipes also celebrate Poe's only complete novel, *The Narrative of Arthur Gordon Pym of Nantucket*.

Each recipe is tied to a quote that relates to a Poe story, including his most recognizable poetry, which accompanies a recipe for raven-shaped black bean cakes: "Once upon a midnight dreary, while I pondered, weak and weary, over many a quaint and curious volume of forgotten lore, while I nodded, nearly napping, suddenly there came a tapping, as of someone gently rapping, rapping at my chamber door. 'Tis some visitor,' I muttered, tapping at my chamber door—only this, and nothing more."—"The Raven"

It is very important to note that there is information and an entire section dedicated to the culinary influence and contributions of those who were brought to the United States through the slave trade. Many shared recipes and customs from their home countries while working tirelessly as street-corner vendors peddling everything, on foot, from penny pies and cakes to milk, pepper-pot soup, and more. They were part of everyday life in Poe's Philadelphia.

Recipes are arranged in five sections, including appetizers and party foods; soups, salads, and sides; main courses; desserts; and sips and mixes.

The recipes are also arranged into five examples of menus for parties and special meals, and they can be rearranged to create even more menus for any occasion. Plan a book club meeting, a date night, or afternoon tea, tailoring your own menu from this assortment of ideas. Consider this a guide, not just for during the Halloween season, but also when there is hunger for history, which is anytime!

Antebellum America in Literature

The American antebellum period (1832–1860) spans the time from the formation of the US government to the outbreak of the American Civil War. Many consider this period in history to be the emergence of American literature. Until this time period, notable authors were largely English authors.

While his contemporaries Henry David Thoreau and Ralph Waldo Emerson rose up as heroes of transcendentalism, Edgar Allan Poe forged a new path in Gothic Romanticism. This genre is distinguished by dark, disturbing narratives of murder, death, torture, and love. Although writer Horace Walpole established the style with his 1764 story "The Castle of Otranto," it was Poe who breathed life into a regular cadence of published stories of this style.

The era is also marked by outstanding literature based on societal reflection, highlighting historical developments and questioning norms, particularly regarding slavery. In 1842, Henry Wadsworth

Longfellow wrote his American classic poem, "The Slave Singing at Midnight." Frederick Douglass wrote *Narrative of the Life of Frederick Douglass, an American Slave* in 1845. Harriet Beecher Stowe's *Uncle Tom's Cabin* was published in 1852.

These stories, and more, still carry weight and influence in the world that is worthy of acknowledging through a historical culinary guide such as this. This book was written with respect for the era during which American history veered in some of the most noteworthy and unprecedented directions.

Poe's Literary Contributions

In 2009, a copy of Edgar Allan Poe's first published work, *Tamerlane and Other Poems*, sold at auction for $662,500. Today, that equals $1.1 million. National Public Radio reported that the sale set a new record in literary bids. Mention Poe's name, however, and most people raise eyebrows, giving a look that hints at disdain. Still, somehow, his influence remains unmatched.

Four distinctly different cities claim him as theirs—Baltimore, New York, Philadelphia, and Richmond, Virginia—and each community maintains a museum dedicated to Poe. Much of this is because Edgar Allan Poe is highly recognized as one of the authors who rose from among the great American literary pioneers who established the new genre of short stories in the mid-nineteenth century. He is also considered chief pioneer of Gothic Romanticism and inventor of the murder mystery in literature. Without him, it's unclear whether there would have been a Sherlock Holmes, a James Bond, or a Columbo.

While people the world over are quite familiar with Poe's dark, often grotesque and deeply disturbing side, fewer are aware of the sentimentality and great sensitivity demonstrated in his writings. From Poe's beautifully constructed and heartfelt letters to his wife, Virginia Clemm, as well as to his aunt and eventual mother-in-law, Maria Clemm, it is clear he was no more fearful of exposing his heart than his dark and dreary side.

His writings may have been so formidable because of the horrifically challenging circumstances of his personal life. Poe was orphaned as an infant and his siblings were separated. Poe's adoptive father, who was a man of extreme wealth, cut him off financially while he was trying to find his footing in his first months at the University of Virginia. As a result, he had to leave school. Poe's wife died at the tender age of twenty-four after an exceedingly trying battle with tuberculosis. His heartbreaking loss is apparent in many of his writings.

This book was written for both those who have studied Poe and those who have yet to delve into his stories. While darkness may dominate Poe's stories, upon a closer reading, there is a light that shines through in the works of this incredible literary artist. This book acknowledges his great works and unparalleled contributions to the literary world with recipes, menus, entertaining ideas, and more.

Cadaverous
APPETIZERS
and
PARTY FOODS

The boundaries which divide life from death are at best shadowy and vague. Who shall say where the one ends, and where the other begins?

—"THE PREMATURE BURIAL"

Boundaries of Life and Death
PARTY DIP: HAM SALAD

1 pound ground ham
1 cup mayonnaise
1 tablespoon pickle relish
¼ teaspoon hot Hungarian paprika, plus more for garnish
¼ teaspoon sea salt
6 sprigs fresh rosemary, for garnish

MAKES 16 SERVINGS

This ham salad is alive with flavors of pickle relish and paprika. Serve this cadaverous delight with House of Usher Party Crackers (page 23).

In a large mixing bowl, add the ham, mayonnaise, relish, paprika, and salt and stir to combine well. Set in refrigerator for at least 1 hour or overnight.

Serve in a small serving dish, garnished with fresh rosemary and a sprinkle of the paprika.

> **HIDEOUS HINT**
>
> *Serve in a skull serving dish and garnish heavily with paprika to enhance the brainlike appearance.*

CADAVEROUS APPETIZERS AND PARTY FOODS

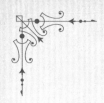

"*Let* him talk," said Dupin, who had not thought it necessary to reply. "Let him discourse; it will ease his conscience. I am satisfied with having defeated him in his own castle."

—"THE MURDERS IN THE RUE MORGUE"

C. August Dupin's CHARCUTERIE BOARD

One 8-ounce sheet frozen pastry dough

1 pound port-wine derby or another cheese that is accented with red wine, cut into bite-size pieces

8 ounces salami

7 mildly spicy pickled cherry peppers

One 8-ounce package cream cheese

8 ounces prosciutto

1 cup blackberry jam

One 16-ounce wheel Brie cheese

1 cup plump, juicy blackberries

8 ounces summer sausage

2 pounds long, thin strips string cheese

7 sprigs fresh sage

6 sprigs fresh curly parsley

Specialty Tools

7 bamboo cocktail skewers

Long cutting board, serving board, or platter

Miniature butcher's cleaver

MAKES 12 SERVINGS

This assortment of meats and cheeses is dedicated to Poe's prolific master detective, C. August Dupin. Poe introduced Dupin in his 1841 short story "The Murders in the Rue Morgue" and featured him in his 1844 short story "The Purloined Letter."

A round of Brie cheese is baked inside pastry dough with blackberry jam. Perfectly round pickled and mildly spicy cherry peppers are stuffed with cooling cream cheese and rolled prosciutto. They resemble the "vulture eyes" Poe made iconic in his 1843 short story "The Tell-Tale Heart." Swirly, winding long bands of string cheese are scattered reminders of the insides of a corpse. Bite-size red meats create blood tones throughout the macabre arrangement.

Set the frozen pastry dough on the countertop for 30 minutes to soften.

While the pastry dough is softening, cut the red wine–stained cheese into bite-size pieces and roll the slices of salami. Slice off the top of each of the peppers and remove the seeds.

Roll the cream cheese into seven $1/2$-inch round balls and place each one in a hollowed cherry pepper. Use the end of a wooden spoon to create a 1-inch-deep hole in each of the balls of cream cheese. Cut the prosciutto into 1-inch pieces and press a piece of prosciutto into each of the balls of cream cheese. Secure each piece with a bamboo cocktail skewer.

Preheat the oven to 350°F. Line a baking sheet with parchment paper.

CONTINUES

CADAVEROUS APPETIZERS AND PARTY FOODS

Spread the pastry dough on the prepared baking sheet. Spread the blackberry jam across the center of the dough. Place the Brie cheese on the pastry dough and wrap the dough all around the edges of the cheese, ensuring the dough is tightly sealed. Bake until the dough is lightly brown and crispy all around on the outside, 35 to 40 minutes. There might be some cheesy jam bubbling up in the seams of the pastry. Remove from the oven and set on the countertop until it is cool enough to handle.

Place the cooled Brie in the center of a large cutting board. Place the cleaver horizontally in the bottom of the cheese.

Arrange the red wine–stained cheese pieces, rolled salami, summer sausage, remaining prosciutto slices, stuffed cherry peppers, remaining blackberries, remaining jam, and strips of string cheese around the Brie pastry and garnish with the sage and parsley. Ingredients that don't fit on the board can be saved for replenishing the board as guests devour the hyper-exquisite treats.

I became once more possessed with a desire of visiting foreign countries; and one day, without acquainting any of my family with my design, I packed up some bundles of such merchandise as was most precious and least bulky, and, engaging a porter to carry them, went with him down to the sea-shore, to await the arrival of any chance vessel that might convey me out of the kingdom into some region which I had not as yet explored.

—SINBAD, "THE THOUSAND-AND-SECOND TALE OF SCHEHERAZADE"

Sinbad the Sailor's ROASTED CARROT *and* BLOOD-ORANGE HUMMUS BOATS

8 carrots, peeled and cut into bite-size pieces

6 tablespoons olive oil, divided

¼ teaspoon sea salt

¼ teaspoon freshly ground multicolored peppercorns

1 cup canned chickpeas

Juice of 1 lemon

1 tablespoon plus 1 teaspoon paprika, plus more for sprinkling

1 teaspoon ground cumin

2 tablespoons tahini

1 clove garlic, coarsely chopped

2 tablespoons blood-orange olive oil or extra-virgin olive oil

2 tablespoons chopped, jarred roasted red peppers

2 tablespoons chopped fresh cilantro

2 small or 1 medium head radicchio

MAKES 16 TO 20 SERVINGS

Poe's 1845 story about Sinbad places him on his eighth and final journey. This plant-forward variation of hummus similarly hails from the Middle East. Add a pop of bright color to any party with this nutritious and delicious treat. Present the hummus in bite-size "boats" made with radicchio leaves. Serve with crudites or small pieces of toasted pita bread or naan bread.

Preheat the oven to 400°F. Line a baking sheet with parchment paper.

In a small mixing bowl, drizzle the carrots with 2 tablespoons of the olive oil. Sprinkle with the salt and pepper and toss until thoroughly coated with the oil and seasonings. Spread on the prepared baking sheet and roast until the carrots are fork-tender, 20 to 25 minutes. Use a spoon to toss them halfway through. Remove the carrots from the oven and set them on the countertop to cool.

While the carrots cool, in a food processor, add the chickpeas, lemon juice, paprika, cumin, tahini, and garlic and process on high speed until creamy. Add the cooled carrots, pulse for several seconds, and then stop to scrape the sides of the food processor to ensure everything is well blended. Add the remaining 4 tablespoons of olive oil to achieve the desired consistency. Depending on the size of your food processor, you may need to blend in batches and then mix together.

Place the hummus in a serving dish. Garnish with the roasted red peppers and cilantro. Add a swirl of blood-orange olive oil to the top. Sprinkle some vibrant red paprika on top. To present as bite-size appetizers, use a spoon to fill the smallest, sturdiest radicchio leaves. Arrange the leaves on a serving platter.

CADAVEROUS APPETIZERS AND PARTY FOODS

I can compare to no earthly sensation more properly than to the afterdream of the reveller upon opium—the bitter lapse into everyday life—the hideous dropping off of the veil.

—"THE FALL OF THE HOUSE OF USHER"

House of Usher Party Crackers: POPPY-SEED CRACKERS *with* LEMON THYME

1½ tablespoons poppy seeds
1½ teaspoons fennel seeds
1½ teaspoons black sesame seeds
1¼ cups all-purpose flour
1 tablespoon sugar
¼ teaspoon sea salt
¼ cup unsalted butter
¼ cup cold water
1 tablespoon fresh or 1½ teaspoons dried lemon thyme or thyme
1 tablespoon extra-virgin olive oil

Specialty Tools
Raven-shaped cookie cutter (shown in 4¾ by 4⅝ inches) (optional)
Pastry brush

MAKES 12 SERVINGS

These lightly crunchy crackers are a cinch to make and only require a few ingredients that are stock items in most pantries. The raven-shaped cookie cutter is optional. These can be cut into long strips or circles. The poppy seeds on their own make these crackers perfect for nibbling at a Poe party. Opium comes from the seedpods of unripe opium poppies.

Preheat the oven to 400°F. Line two baking sheets with parchment paper.

In a small bowl, use your fingertips to mix the seeds together. In a large mixing bowl, add the flour, sugar, salt, butter, water, lemon thyme, and the seeds. Mix the dough until well combined. The dough should be moist, but not sticky. Form the dough into a ball and place it on the countertop. Use a rolling pin to roll the dough to ⅛ inch thick.

Use the raven-shaped cookie cutter to cut out the dough. The first batch will produce eight raven shapes. Use your hands to mix together the dough remnants, forming them into a ball. Roll the dough out and use the cookie cutter to make four more raven shapes.

Place the crackers on the prepared baking sheets. Using a pastry brush, brush a little bit of the extra-virgin olive oil on top of each raven, just covering each one lightly.

Put the raven crackers in the oven and bake them until they are cooked through and dark around the edges and tops, 10 to 12 minutes. Watch them closely to avoid burning. When they are finished baking, remove the raven crackers from the oven and set them on the countertop to cool.

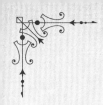

And all-around rare flowers did blow. The wild rose pale perfumed the gale and the queenly lily adown.

—"FOREST REVERIE"

Forest Reverie BUTTER BOARD

2 cups red and/or black grapes

1 teaspoon extra-virgin olive oil

1 tablespoon fresh thyme leaves (if available, lemon thyme)

3 teaspoons coarse salt

6 tablespoons unsalted butter, softened

2 tablespoons crushed, dried rose petals

1 tablespoon coarsely chopped pistachios

Zest of 1 lemon

3 to 5 fresh spruce or rosemary tips

MAKES 12 SERVINGS

Roasted grapes take center stage in this butter board, surrounded by rose petals, chopped dry-roasted pistachios, and spruce or rosemary tips. Although the truth of her stories remains challenged by naysayers, Poe biographer Susan Archer Talley Weiss claimed she sent a delivery of her family's homegrown grapes to Poe's hotel room each morning during his last visit to Richmond in the summer of 1849. Scoop up a bite of this buttery treat with House of Usher Party Crackers (page 23).

Preheat the oven to 425°F.

In a small mixing bowl, add the grapes, drizzle with the oil, and sprinkle with half of the thyme and 1½ teaspoons of the salt. Toss to coat. Place the grapes in a small baking dish and roast for 15 to 20 minutes, or until the grapes have roasted enough to create a light, purple sauce and the skins appear cooked. Remove them from the oven and set them on the countertop to cool. Reserve the sauce to sprinkle over the butter board later.

On a platter or a cheese board, use a butter knife to spread the butter across the board. When the grapes are cool, use your hands to arrange the grapes throughout the butter. Scatter the rose petals, pistachios, remaining ½ tablespoon thyme, remaining 1½ teaspoons salt, and lemon zest over the grapes. Sprinkle just a few drops of the grape sauce lightly across the board. Place the spruce tips around the edges of the board.

℞emoving the third case, we discovered and took out the body itself. We had expected to find it, as usual, enveloped in frequent rolls, or bandages, of linen; but in place of these we found a sort of sheath, made of papyrus, and coated with a layer of plaster, thickly gilt and painted.

—"SOME WORDS WITH A MUMMY"

Some Words with a Mummy APPETIZER

One 17.3-ounce package frozen puff pastry dough
8 ounces summer sausage
8 ounces salami
8 ounces prosciutto
One 7-ounce tub Gouda cheese spread

MAKES 20 SERVINGS

This delicious, shared appetizer is puff pastry dough filled with sausage, salami, and prosciutto, and a flavored spreadable cheese. The dough is cut into thin strips that, when wrapped around the pastry-dough legs, arms, and head, give the appearance of a mummy.

Preheat the oven to 375°F. Line a baking sheet with parchment paper.

Remove the frozen puff pastry from the freezer and set it on the countertop for 15 minutes. When the pastry dough is still chilled but no longer frozen, use a knife to cut the dough into five 6-inch-long rectangle shapes for the arms, legs, and midsection and one 1½-inch circle for the head. Cut the remaining dough into ¼-inch-wide strips, 4 to 5 inches long.

On the prepared baking sheet, arrange the rectangle and round shapes in the form of a human mummy. Place the meat on top, in layers. Use a tablespoon to evenly place six to eight spoonfuls of the cheese on top of the meats. Arrange the long strips on top of the meats and cheese, twisting and intertwining the strips to resemble mummy bandages.

Bake until lightly browned all around, 30 to 35 minutes. Remove from the oven and serve warm.

HIDEOUS HINT

Give the mummy two pimento-stuffed olive eyes so he can see whom he is having words with. Present to guests with a tiny butcher's cleaver set in the mummy.

CADAVEROUS APPETIZERS AND PARTY FOODS

Upon awaking, and stretching forth an arm, I found beside me a loaf and a pitcher with water. I was too much exhausted to reflect upon this circumstance, but ate and drank with avidity. A slight noise attracted my notice, and, looking to the floor, I saw several enormous rats traversing it. They had issued from the well, which lay just within view to my right. Even then, while I gazed, they came up in troops, hurriedly, with ravenous eyes, allured by the scent of the meat. From this it required much effort and attention to scare them away.

—"THE PIT AND THE PENDULUM"

The Pit and the Pendulum Bread: GINGERBREAD

Cooking spray
2 cups all-purpose flour
1 teaspoon baking soda
1 tablespoon freshly grated ginger
½ teaspoon freshly grated nutmeg
¼ teaspoon ground cloves
¼ teaspoon ground cinnamon
¼ teaspoon pink Himalayan salt
½ cup unsalted butter, softened
½ cup dark brown sugar
1 vanilla bean pod
½ cup molasses
2 large eggs
1 cup buttermilk
4 or 5 drops black food coloring, or more as desired
Powdered sugar, for dusting

Specialty Tools
9-by-5-inch (1½-pound) bread loaf pan
Rat stencil or cookie cutter
1 Cinnamon Red Hots candy for the eye, plus extra to spread around the base of the gingerbread (optional)

MAKES 12 SERVINGS

A light dusting of powdered sugar over a stencil in the shape of a rat gives this loaf of gingerbread the Spanish Inquisition (1478–1834) vibe Poe re-created in his 1842 short story "The Pit and The Pendulum." You can almost see the "venomous eyes."

Preheat the oven to 350°F. Coat a loaf pan with cooking spray.

In a large mixing bowl, add the flour, baking soda, ginger, nutmeg, cloves, cinnamon, and salt and whisk to combine. Set aside.

In the bowl of a stand mixer or in a large mixing bowl if using a handheld mixer, cream the butter and brown sugar on medium speed. Use a paring knife to open the vanilla bean pod and scrape out the seeds inside. Add the seeds and the molasses to the bowl and beat to combine, then add the eggs, one at a time, and beat to combine.

Working in thirds, add the flour mixture to the butter mixture, alternating with the buttermilk. Add the food coloring. Blend until combined.

Spread the batter in the prepared loaf pan and bake until a toothpick or knife inserted into the center comes out clean, about 60 to 80 minutes. Remove from the oven and place on the countertop to cool.

When the gingerbread is cool, place the rat stencil on top and sift the powdered sugar over the top to create the shape of a rat. If using a cookie cutter, place the cookie cutter on parchment paper and use a pen to trace around the cookie cutter. Cut out the shape and tape it to the top of the cookie cutter. Seal the parchment paper all around to ensure no powdered sugar gets through a crack.

Serve with a pitcher of water.

28 CADAVEROUS APPETIZERS AND PARTY FOODS

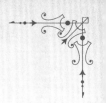

Hear the sledges with the bells—Silver bells! What a world of merriment their melody foretells! How they tinkle, tinkle, tinkle, in the icy air of night!!
—"THE BELLS"

Icy Air of Night FRUIT PLATTER

Fruit Platter
3 kiwano melons, cut into quarters

3 dragon fruits, thinly sliced

3 kiwi, halved and cut into decorative shapes

24 large blueberries

24 lychees, peeled and pitted (optional)

Fruit Dip
One 16-ounce jar marshmallow creme

One 8-ounce package cream cheese, softened

1 teaspoon maraschino cherry juice

4 drops red food coloring, or more as desired

Specialty Tool
Extra-large silicone skull cake pan

MAKES 20 SERVINGS

The lifelike ice "skull-pture" at the center of this fruit arrangement reflects the icy air of night that Poe wrote about in his 1849 poem "The Bells." He submitted the poem three times to *Sartain's Union Magazine* until it was finally published one month after his death. Vibrant colors of dragon fruit, vulture-eye bites (lychees and blueberries), kiwano melons, and kiwi dazzle in this arrangement. There is no limit to the number and variety of fruits to include. A dark-red cherry dip makes these fruits irresistible.

To make the ice "skull-pture": Place a cake pan in a large roasting pan. Place bunched-up aluminum foil all around the cake pan to steady it. Place the pans in the freezer and use a cup to fill the cake pan with water. Freeze until solid, ideally overnight. Remove from the freezer and take the ice form out of the silicone mold. Place 8 cups of ice cubes in a large glass bowl and stand both sides of the skull up, supported by the ice cubes. The sides will freeze together to form a solid block, which can be transferred to the platter.

Artfully arrange favorite fruits around the ice skull-pture. Any fruits will work, but dragon fruit, vulture-eye bites (lychees stuffed with blueberries), kiwano melons, kiwi, and more cast an appetizing haze a gloom to this arrangement. A dark-red cherry dip makes these fruits irresistible.

To make optional lychee eyeballs: Place a blueberry in the center of each lychee. Scatter the eyes around the display and place them as eyes in the ice skull-pture to complete the ghoulish display.

To make the dip: In the bowl of a stand mixer or in a large mixing bowl if using a handheld mixer, beat all the ingredients on medium speed until well blended. Serve on the side.

HIDEOUS HINT

Create blood spatter on the fruit platter using a spoon and a little cherry juice.

He had the eye of a vulture—a pale blue eye, with a film over it. Whenever it fell upon me, my blood ran cold; and so by degrees—very gradually—I made up my mind to take the life of the old man, and thus rid myself of the eye forever.

—"THE TELL-TALE HEART"

Vulture-Eye DEVILED EGGS

12 large eggs
4 drops red food coloring
1 cup mayonnaise
½ cup Dijon mustard
¼ teaspoon sea salt
½ teaspoon freshly ground multicolored peppercorns
1 head oakleaf lettuce, leaves separated
¼ teaspoon hot Hungarian paprika, plus extra for garnish
¼ cup chopped fresh parsley, for garnish
12 black olives, pitted and halved

Specialty Tool
Piping bag with medium round tip

MAKES 12 SERVINGS

With beet-stain veins and three-dimensional eyeball fillings, these deviled eggs resemble the "vulture eye" the narrator describes in Poe's 1843 story "The Tell-Tale Heart."

Place the eggs in a large heavy saucepan over high heat, add water to cover by 1 to 2 inches, and bring to a boil. Remove from the heat, cover, and let stand for 10 minutes. Transfer the eggs to a bowl of ice water and let stand for 15 minutes to stop the cooking.

Tap the eggs on the counter to make cracks in the shells. Fill a medium bowl halfway with water and add the red food coloring. Place the eggs in the water and the bowl in the refrigerator for at least 1 hour.

Remove the eggs from the refrigerator and peel them. Halve each egg lengthwise. Remove the yolk from each egg, being careful not to break the whites, and place the yolks in a large bowl. Set the whites aside. Using a fork, mash the yolks. Add the mayonnaise, mustard, salt, and pepper and mix until thoroughly combined.

Transfer the egg-yolk filling to a piping bag fitted with a medium round tip. Alternatively, you can use a large plastic storage bag with ½ inch of a bottom corner cut off. Roll the sides of the bag down so that you can fill it at the open end. Fill the bag with the mixture, roll the sides back up, and press the mixture into the open corner.

Line a large platter with the lettuce leaves. Arrange the egg whites around the platter of lettuce leaves. Pipe the filling into the wells of the egg whites. Garnish with a sprinkle of paprika and fresh parsley. Top each deviled egg with an olive half to create the eyes.

CADAVEROUS APPETIZERS AND PARTY FOODS

(*H*ousehold) management is an art that may be acquired by any woman of good sense and tolerable memory. If, unfortunately, she has been bred in a family where domestic business is the work of chance, she will have many difficulties to encounter; but a determined resolution to obtain this valuable knowledge will enable her to surmount all obstacles.

—MARY RANDOLPH, *THE VIRGINIA HOUSEWIFE*

TAVERN BISCUITS

4 cups all-purpose flour
1 cup sugar
1 cup butter
Pinch of ground mace
Pinch of ground nutmeg
⅓ cup brandy

MAKES 12 SERVINGS

Edgar Allan Poe was living near Mary Randolph in Richmond, Virginia, while she wrote the groundbreaking 1825 cookbook *The Virginia Housewife*. Mary's book remains one of the most important culinary references today. It features many classic recipes—called "receipts" at the time—including this recipe for the very popular Tavern Biscuits. They are like savory cookies. While these biscuits are a satisfying snack or a flavorful bite, they are customarily dry. This is an adaptation of Mary Randolph's recipe.

Preheat the oven to 375°F.

Line a large baking sheet with parchment paper.

In a large mixing bowl, add the flour, sugar, butter, mace, and nutmeg and whisk to combine. Add the brandy and use your hands to mix to combine. Add more brandy if too dry; add more flour if too wet.

Knead the dough in the bowl or on the countertop until the dough comes together into a ball.

With a rolling pin, roll it out to ¼-inch thick and use a 1½-inch round cookie cutter to cut out biscuits. Gather the dough remnants together, re-roll, and cut out more shapes.

Place on the prepared baking sheet and bake until the biscuits are lightly browned around the edges, about 15 to 20 minutes. Watch these closely as they bake quickly.

The wine sparkled in his eyes and the bells jingled. My own fancy grew warm with the Médoc. We had passed through long walls of piled skeletons, with casks and puncheons intermingling, into the inmost recesses of the catacombs. I paused again, and this time I made bold to seize Fortunato by an arm above the elbow.

—MONTRESOR, "THE CASK OF AMONTILLADO"

Fortunato's STUFFED MÉDOC MUSHROOMS

1 tablespoon unsalted butter, softened

2 tablespoons extra-virgin olive oil

2 tablespoons diced shallot

24 button mushrooms

1 tablespoon diced red bell pepper

1 tablespoon plain breadcrumbs

¼ teaspoon dry mustard

1 cup chopped fresh parsley tops (no stems)

½ cup Médoc wine (merlot)

Juice from ½ lemon

½ teaspoon freshly ground peppercorns

¼ teaspoon sea salt

2 tablespoons grated Emmentaler cheese (can substitute mozzarella)

MAKES 12 SERVINGS

HIDEOUS HINT

Before baking, top each stuffed mushroom cap with curly, spiny squid tentacles.

Poe described the mushrooms overgrowing the House of Usher in one of his most popular works, the 1839 short story "The Fall of the House of Usher": "Minute fungi overspread the whole exterior, hanging in a fine tangled web-work from the eaves. Yet all this was apart from any extraordinary dilapidation." These stuffed mushrooms are made with traditional ingredients, including chopped mushroom stems, which are simmered low and slow in a Médoc wine. Médoc is a red wine, such as merlot or cabernet sauvignon, from the Médoc region in France.

Preheat the oven to 350°F. Grease a 9-inch pie plate or an 8-inch square baking dish with the butter.

In a frying pan over medium heat, heat the oil. Add the shallots. Pull out the stems from the mushrooms, chop them, and add to the shallots. Set the caps aside. Add the bell pepper, breadcrumbs, mustard, ⅔ cup of the parsley, Médoc wine, lemon juice, pepper, and salt. Stir to combine and let simmer, low and slow, stirring occasionally, for 30 minutes.

Brush off the mushroom caps to remove any soil and arrange them in the prepared baking dish, top-side down, so that the openings are facing up. Use a spoon to stuff the mushroom mixture into each mushroom cap. Stuff as much of the mixture into each mushroom as the mushroom will hold. Sprinkle the mushrooms with the Emmentaler cheese and bake until the stuffing and the mushrooms become baked together and the mushrooms turn much darker, 30 to 40 minutes.

Remove from the oven and serve hot, sprinkled with the remaining ⅓ cup of fresh parsley.

With the unutterable ecstacies of butternuts, gingerbread, and milk and water!
—"POLITIAN"

A thousand years would fail to force me from my jailor.
—"THE PIT AND THE PENDULUM"

PATATAS BRAVAS

Potatoes
4 small red potatoes, unpeeled
1 tablespoon extra-virgin olive oil
¼ teaspoon sea salt
¼ teaspoon freshly ground pepper

Sauce
3 tablespoons extra-virgin olive oil
1 clove garlic, minced
4.5 ounces tomato paste (a heaping ½ cup)
¼ teaspoon hot Hungarian paprika
¼ teaspoon red pepper flakes
¼ teaspoon sea salt
¼ teaspoon freshly ground black pepper
1 cup vegetable broth
1 teaspoon red wine vinegar
1 teaspoon cornstarch
¼ cup chopped fresh curly parsley or cilantro

MAKES 4 SERVINGS

Patatas Bravas is one of the classic tapas dishes of Spain, which is where Poe's 1842 short story "The Pit and the Pendulum" is set. Carve eyes and round mouths into roasted red potatoes to make them resemble the ghouls and spirits that remain in the Medina castle, where so many souls suffered dreadfully during the Spanish Inquisition (1478–1834).

Preheat the oven to 375°F.

In a large mixing bowl, add the potatoes, drizzle with the oil, and sprinkle with the salt and pepper. Toss to coat the potatoes in the oil and seasonings. Place the potatoes in a 9-inch square baking dish, propping them up with crumpled foil, and roast until they are fork-tender, 40 to 45 minutes. Remove the potatoes from the oven and set them on the countertop.

While the potatoes are roasting, in a large saucepan over medium heat, heat the olive oil. Add the garlic and sauté for 1 to 2 minutes. Add the tomato paste, paprika, red pepper flakes, salt, and pepper and whisk to combine. Add the broth and vinegar, whisking continuously. Bring to a boil, then decrease the heat to medium-low and simmer until lightly thickened, about 15 minutes. Sprinkle in the cornstarch, whisking continuously until the cornstarch is completely dissolved. Simmer for 5 minutes. Remove from the heat and set on the countertop.

On a small platter or large plate, spread the sauce. Arrange the potatoes on the sauce. Garnish with the parsley. Serve with a large spoon for guests to share the dish, Spanish tapas style.

HIDEOUS HINT

When the potatoes are cool enough to handle, use a paring knife to carve out circles to make eyes and mouths. Slice ¼ inch off the bottom of each potato so it stands straight to display the face.

At midnight he unearths the coffin, opens it, and is in the act of detaching the hair, when he is arrested by the unclosing of the beloved eyes. In fact, the lady had been buried alive. Vitality had not altogether departed, and she was aroused by the caresses of her lover from the lethargy which had been mistaken for death.

—"THE PREMATURE BURIAL"

Alarum Premature Burial FRUIT-PASTRY BITES

Coffins
One 17.3-ounce package frozen puff pastry

Filling
1 cup cream cheese, softened
2 cups fresh raspberries or chopped strawberries
1 teaspoon fresh lemon juice
¼ teaspoon sugar
¼ teaspoon pink Himalayan sea salt

Specialty Tools
6-inch coffin-shaped cookie cutter (can substitute a rectangle-shaped cutter or cut the dough into rectangles using a knife)
4 bamboo cocktail skewers or toothpicks

Garnish
4 maraschino cherries, stems intact

MAKES 4 SERVINGS

Philadelphians—and, eventually, readers around the world—ravenously devoured Poe's story "The Premature Burial" in *The Philadelphia Dollar Newspaper* in 1844. Poe loved breathing life into rarely used words and invented nearly a thousand of his own words and phrases. One of those words, alarum, relates to the word alarm. "The Premature Burial" story raised much alarum of being buried alive. Some coffin makers purportedly started making coffins with alarms inside in case they were needed due to premature burial. These sweet treats are filled with fluffy whipped cream cheese and berries and the cherries represent alarm buttons.

Preheat the oven to 350°F. Line a baking sheet with parchment paper.

Remove the frozen puff pastry from the freezer and set on the countertop for 15 minutes. When the pastry dough is still chilled but no longer frozen, place a coffin-shaped cookie cutter on top and cut around the outside with a paring knife. Cut out a total of eight coffin-shaped pastry puffs to make the tops and bottoms for four coffins. Cut 8 small strips to form the crosses on top.

Place the puff pastry cutouts on the prepared baking sheet, decorate the top of four of them with crosses, and bake until they are lightly browned all around, 15 to 20 minutes. Watch them closely; be careful not to overbake. Remove the pastry puffs from the oven and set them on the countertop to cool.

To make the filling: In a stand mixer or in a large mixing bowl if using a handheld mixer, beat all the ingredients on medium speed until well blended.

Use an offset spatula to spread the cream cheese mixture on the bottom pastry puffs. Cover each one with a coffin "lid." Use scissors to remove the bottom 1 inch of the cocktail skewers or toothpicks and secure a cherry in the top right corner of each coffin.

CADAVEROUS APPETIZERS AND PARTY FOODS

Immensely tall trunks of trees, gray and leafless, rose up in endless succession as far as the eye could reach. Their roots were concealed in wide-spreading morasses, whose dreary water lay intensely black, still, and altogether terrible, beneath. And the strange trees seemed endowed with a human vitality, and waving to and fro their skeleton arms, were crying to the silent waters for mercy, in the shrill and piercing accents of the most acute agony and despair.

—THE NARRATIVE OF ARTHUR GORDON PYM OF NANTUCKET

Arthur Gordon Pym's
BLACK-TREE CANDY BARK

One 11.5-ounce bag milk chocolate chips

1 tablespoon vegetable oil

3 ounces graveyard-themed cake decorating sprinkles (tiny edible coffins, tombstones, femur bones, etc.)

3 ounces eyeball cake-decorating confetti

4 sprigs fresh rosemary

4 sprigs fresh sage

MAKES 20 SERVINGS

This milk-chocolate bark is decorated with candy skulls, eyeballs, and other ghastly treats. Guests can use wooden mallets to break the slab apart in pieces to enjoy as a sweet snack after a morose meal.

Place the chocolate chips in a microwave-safe bowl and microwave for 30 seconds. Stir, and microwave for 30 seconds more. Continue until the chocolate is just melted. Add the oil and stir to combine thoroughly. Spread the melted chocolate on a 12-inch platter.

In a medium bowl, combine the cake decorating sprinkles and confetti and stir. Spread the sprinkles across the chocolate before it hardens. Set aside to cool and set for at least 1 hour. Garnish with the herbs arranged around the platter. Break up into a few pieces for guests.

CADAVEROUS APPETIZERS AND PARTY FOODS

Edgar, I haven't forgotten you.
—"THE POE TOASTER"

The Poe Toaster's
ANCHOVY TOAST POINTS

2 tablespoons unsalted butter, softened

1 teaspoon drained and finely chopped canned anchovies

¼ teaspoon fresh lemon juice

¼ teaspoon lemon zest

¼ teaspoon freshly ground multicolored peppercorns

3 large pieces bread, toasted

2 tablespoons chopped fresh dill

1 lemon slice, cut into thirds

MAKES 4 TO 6 SERVINGS

This was the only known message penned by the mysterious person who made a perennial visit to Poe's grave in Baltimore for over half a century, becoming beloved the world over as "The Poe Toaster." He left this message behind after his visit in 2001, shortly before the Ravens and the Giants faced off in Superbowl XXXV.

These anchovy toast points are like the anchovy toast on menus in the middle of the nineteenth century at trendy places like the Parker House in Boston.

In a small bowl, add the butter, anchovies, lemon juice and zest, and pepper and stir to combine.

Trim the crust from the edges of the toast and cut the toast into quarters. Use a butter knife to smear a little of the butter mixture on each of the toast points.

Garnish with the fresh dill and lemon slices.

CADAVEROUS APPETIZERS AND PARTY FOODS

Once upon a midnight dreary, while I pondered, weak and weary, over many a quaint and curious volume of forgotten lore, while I nodded, nearly napping, suddenly there came a tapping, as of someone gently rapping, rapping at my chamber door. "Tis some visitor," I muttered, "tapping at my chamber door—only this and nothing more."

—"THE RAVEN"

ROASTED APRICOTS *and* BANANAS RAVEN FOOD

1 pound dried banana chips
10 ounces dried apricots
1 pound dried cherries
1 pound dry-roasted peanuts
1 pound honey-roasted sesame sticks
½ cup honey

MAKES 20 SERVINGS

Poe's 1845 poem "The Raven" remains so popular that guests will love to munch on a raven-themed snack. This mix of banana chips, dried apricots, cherries, nuts, and sesame sticks roasted in honey would be the perfect food for a hungry raven.

Preheat the oven to 350°F.

Place all of the ingredients except the honey in an 18-inch roasting pan. Drizzle the honey over the ingredients and use a large spoon to stir the honey throughout. Bake for 10 minutes and stir. Return to the oven for 10 more minutes. Remove from the oven and set on the countertop to cool.

HIDEOUS HINT

Give your guests a gift to take home with them as a souvenir of your ghastly gathering. Fill clear plastic skull-shaped jars with the raven food for each guest. Tie the recipe to the jar lid with a black ribbon.

CADAVEROUS APPETIZERS AND PARTY FOODS

Last night, for supper, we had the nicest tea you ever drank, strong and hot—wheat bread and rye bread—cheese—tea-cakes . . . Everything in the greatest profusion.

—EDGAR ALLAN POE, LETTER HOME FROM NEW YORK TO
HIS AUNT AND MOTHER-IN-LAW, MARIA CLEMM, APRIL 7, 1844

TEA CAKES

1 cup sugar
1 cup butter, softened
3 eggs, at room temperature
1 vanilla bean pod
3 cups all-purpose flour
2 tablespoons baking powder
¼ teaspoon pink Himalayan sea salt

MAKES 12 SERVINGS

This is an easy, basic recipe for classic tea cakes like Poe would have eaten during his 1844 visit to New York.

Preheat the oven to 375°F. Line a baking sheet with parchment paper.

In a stand mixer or in a large bowl if using a handheld mixer, cream the sugar and butter on medium-high speed until fluffy, 6 to 7 minutes. One at a time, add the eggs, beating well after each addition. Use a paring knife to open the vanilla bean pod and scrape out the seeds into the eggs and butter. Beat until combined.

In a separate bowl, mix together the flour, baking powder, and salt. Add to the butter mixture and beat until combined.

Use a large serving spoon to scoop up the dough and place spoonfuls on the baking sheet 2 to 3 inches apart. Bake the cakes until they are browned around the edges, 6 to 7 minutes. Remove the cakes from the oven and set them on a wire rack to cool.

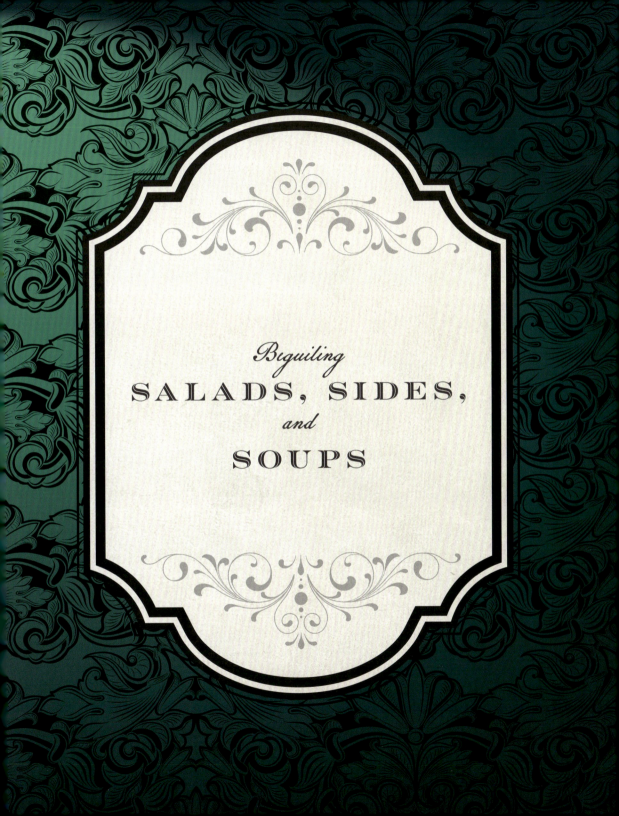

Beguiling
SALADS, SIDES,
and
SOUPS

A cadaverousness of complexion; an eye large, liquid, and very luminous . . .
—"THE FALL OF THE HOUSE OF USHER"

Cadaver RICE

4 small butternut squash
2 tablespoons olive oil
1 large shallot, diced
8 ounces sliced mushrooms, chopped
¼ teaspoon salt
¼ teaspoon freshly ground black peppercorns
2 cups black rice, prepared according to package directions

MAKES 4 SERVINGS

This rice is mixed with a medley of sautéed mushrooms and roasted butternut squash. Serve this in a large squash as a centerpiece to be passed around the table or give each guest their own individual small carved squash.

Preheat the oven to 375°F.

Place the squash in a roasting pan and roast for 1 hour.

While the squash is roasting, prepare the mushrooms and shallots. In a medium saucepan over medium heat, heat the olive oil. Add the shallots and sauté for 1 minute. Add the mushrooms, salt, and pepper and continue to sauté.

Remove the squash from the oven and set on the countertop to cool. When the squash are cool enough to handle, cut off the tops and scoop out the seeds. Cut the squash from the tops into 1-inch square pieces.

In a large mixing bowl, combine the shallots, mushrooms, and squash cubes with the prepared rice. Fill each squash with the rice mixture and serve.

HIDEOUS HINT

For a festive touch, you can carve large, luminous eyes and a mouth in the roasted squashes, similar to a jack-o'-lantern.

BEGUILING SALADS, SIDES, AND SOUPS

ewildered, I flew to the ottoman, and endeavored to arouse the sleeper to a sense of the startling intelligence. But his limbs were rigid—his lips were livid—his lately beaming eyes were riveted in death.

—"THE ASSIGNATION"

The Assignation SALAD

This salad showcases autumn stone fruit, roasted apple, peppers, and lettuce. The "beaming eyes riveted in death" are roasted tomatillo peppers filled with cream cheese balls stuffed with olives. Roasted poblano pepper pesto adds a bit of heat.

Salad
2 large peaches or plums
1 large Red Delicious apple
1 fennel bulb
6 tomatillo peppers
1 large red bell pepper
2 large poblano peppers
3 tablespoons extra-virgin olive oil
¼ teaspoon sea salt
¼ teaspoon freshly ground peppercorns
12 ounces spring mix lettuce
One 8-ounce ball fresh mozzarella, sliced into ¼-inch rounds
5 ounces cream cheese, softened
5 black olives

Roasted Poblano Pepper Dressing
2 roasted poblano peppers (from the roasted vegetables for the salad)
3 tablespoons extra-virgin olive oil
½ teaspoon fresh lemon juice
¼ teaspoon sea salt
¼ teaspoon freshly ground peppercorns

MAKES 6 SERVINGS

Preheat the oven to 375°F. Line a baking sheet with parchment paper.

Cut the peaches or plums into quarters and remove the pits. Slice five very thin slices from the apple. Coarsely chop the fennel bulb into 3-inch pieces. Use a paring knife to remove the tops of the tomatillo peppers and cut ½-inch-deep slits into each. Slice ¼-inch-thick rings from the red bell pepper, removing the seeds.

In a large mixing bowl, toss the peaches or plums, apple, fennel, tomatillos, red bell pepper, and poblano peppers in the olive oil, salt, and pepper.

Arrange the ingredients on the prepared baking sheet and roast until they are lightly browned around the edges and softened all around, for about 30 minutes. Remove the baking sheet from the oven and set it on the countertop until the ingredients are cool enough to handle.

Arrange the lettuce on a platter. Spread the roasted fruits and vegetables on top. Place ¼-inch-thick round slices of mozzarella cheese on top.

Use your hands to form five ½-inch balls of cream cheese and place one into each tomatillo pepper. Press an olive into each cream cheese ball. Arrange the peppers on the salad. Combine all the ingredients for the dressing, then dress the salad or serve the dressing on the side.

HIDEOUS HINT
Use a paring knife to carve eyes and mouths into the cheese slices.

BEGUILING SALADS, SIDES, AND SOUPS

The margin of the river, and of the many dazzling rivulets that glided through devious ways into its channel, as well as the spaces that extended from the margins away down into the depths of the streams until they reached the bed of pebbles at the bottom,—these spots, not less than the whole surface of the valley, from the river to the mountains that girdled it in, were carpeted all by a soft green grass, thick, short, perfectly even, and vanilla-perfumed, but so besprinkled throughout with the yellow buttercup, the white daisy, the purple violet, and the ruby-red asphodel, that its exceeding beauty spoke to our hearts in loud tones, of the love and of the glory of God.

—"ELEANORA"

Vanilla-Perfumed INDIAN PUDDING

1 tablespoon unsalted butter, softened
3 cups whole milk
½ cup cornmeal
1 tablespoon molasses
2 small eggs
1 vanilla bean pod, scraped
¼ cup sugar
½ teaspoon freshly grated ginger
½ teaspoon ground cinnamon
½ teaspoon freshly ground nutmeg
¼ teaspoon sea salt
¼ teaspoon freshly ground multicolored peppercorns

MAKES 8 SERVINGS

In his 1842 short story "Eleanora," Poe wrote of a vanilla-perfumed valley. Around the time that he wrote "Eleanora," trendy restaurants served Indian pudding. Lightly laden with autumnal aromas of nutmeg and cinnamon, this recipe for Indian pudding gets its bright, airy scent from the vanilla. Indian pudding is made like the traditional English puddings that early American colonists made, but instead of flour, it is made with something colonists had only just learned of: cornmeal.

Preheat the oven 375°F. Grease a 9-inch round pie pan with the butter.

In a medium saucepan over medium-high heat, scald the milk. Add the cornmeal and molasses and whisk to combine. Stir until thickened.

In a mixing bowl, add the eggs, vanilla bean seeds, sugar, ginger, cinnamon, nutmeg, salt, and pepper and stir to combine. Add the milk and cornmeal mixture and stir to combine.

Fill the prepared pie pan with the pudding mixture and bake until the edges start to firm and brown, and a knife inserted in the middle comes out clean, about 45 minutes. The pudding will be jiggly in the center when removed from the oven, but will become firmer after cooling.

BEGUILING SALADS, SIDES, AND SOUPS

The thousand injuries of Fortunato I had borne as best I could, but when he ventured upon insult I swore revenge.
—"THE CASK OF AMONTILLADO"

Catacombs ROASTED ZUCCHINI and BLACK RICE *with* BELL PEPPERS

1 large zucchini

2 tablespoons extra-virgin olive oil

¼ teaspoon salt

¼ teaspoon freshly ground peppercorns

1 large red bell pepper, seeded and diced

¼ cup diced red onion

2 cups black rice, prepared according to package directions

MAKES 4 SERVINGS

These roasted zucchini slices, arranged on a bed of black rice, look like the faces of the catacombs in Poe's 1846 short story "The Cask of Amontillado."

Preheat the oven to 375°F. Line a baking sheet with parchment paper.

Cut seven ¼-inch-thick round slices from the zucchini. Use a paring knife to carve eyes and mouths in the zucchini slices. In a large mixing bowl, add the zucchini, 1 tablespoon of the olive oil, and half each of the salt and pepper. Toss to coat the zucchini. Place the zucchini on the prepared baking sheet and roast until the slices begin to look browned and slightly shriveled, about 30 minutes. Remove from the oven and set on the countertop.

While the zucchini is roasting, prepare the bell peppers and onions. In a saucepan over medium heat, heat the remaining 1 tablespoon oil. Add the bell peppers and onions and sauté for 5 minutes. Add the remaining salt and pepper and stir to combine.

In a large mixing bowl, combine the rice, onions, and bell peppers. Spread the rice mixture on a serving platter. Arrange the zucchini slices across the bed of black rice, like faces looking out from against the ghastly walls of the catacombs.

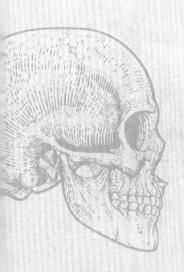

BEGUILING SALADS, SIDES, AND SOUPS

What ho! What ho! this fellow is dancing mad; He hath been bitten by the Tarantula.
—"THE GOLD-BUG"

SOUTH CAROLINA PEACHES *and* PORK *Tarantula* PULL-APART BREAD

6 bacon strips, cut into ½-inch pieces

Three 8-ounce packages frozen crescent rolls, thawed according to package directions

6 ounces pork salami, cut into ½-inch pieces

1 cup chopped cling peaches

2 cups mini mozzarella cheese balls

½ cup unsalted butter, melted

1 tablespoon diced red onion

¼ teaspoon salt

¼ teaspoon freshly ground black peppercorns

2 egg whites

6 sprigs fresh sage

6 sprigs fresh rosemary

MAKES 20 SERVINGS

HIDEOUS HINT

Use two pimento-stuffed olives to give the tarantula eyes.

Poe's 1842 story "The Gold-Bug" is set on Sullivan's Island in South Carolina. This tarantula-shaped pull-apart bread is made with some of the foods that are popular in South Carolina, including peaches and pork (bacon).

Preheat the oven to 375°F. Line two baking sheets with parchment paper.

Place the bacon in a 9-inch square baking dish and bake until golden brown and crispy, about 20 minutes or until it reaches desired crispness. Remove from the oven and place the bacon on a plate with paper towels to absorb residual grease. Blot the top of the bacon with the paper towels.

Cut the thawed dough into 1-inch pieces, reserving one-quarter. Set aside in a large bowl. From the reserved dough, cut four ½-inch by 6-inch strips with a paring knife. Add the bacon, salami, peaches, cheese, butter, onion, salt, and pepper. Stir until well combined and the pieces of dough are thoroughly covered in the melted butter.

On one of the baking sheets, use an 8-inch round bowl to form a dome with some of the bread mixture. Use a 6-inch bowl to form a smaller dome with the remaining bread mixture. On the other baking sheet, form four 2-inch-wide strips that run the length of the baking sheet.

Beat the egg whites lightly in a small bowl and use a pastry brush to cover the bread on both baking sheets with the egg white.

Bake both domes until golden brown all around, especially around the edges, about 45 minutes. Remove from the oven. The thin strips will probably bake faster than the bread domes, so watch carefully.

Place cardboard on a tabletop and cover with two layers of parchment paper. Place the large dome (tarantula body) in the center. Position the small dome so it forms the spider's head. Cut the four long strips of bread in half to make eight tarantula legs. Arrange four legs on each side of the large dome. Arrange the sage and rosemary around the tarantula to create a setting like Sullivan's Island.

BEGUILING SALADS, SIDES, AND SOUPS

As I stared out into the abyss, I realized that life is a constant battle between hope and despair.

—THE NARRATIVE OF ARTHUR GORDON PYM OF NANTUCKET

Arthur Gordon Pym's CLAM CHOWDER

Two 6.5-ounce cans clams
3 lemons
1 cup chopped applewood-smoked bacon or regular bacon
¼ cup diced red onion
1 large stalk celery, finely diced
1 cup peeled and diced russet potatoes
1 small clove garlic, minced
1 cup water
1½ cups vegetable broth
¼ teaspoon sea salt
1 teaspoon freshly ground multicolored peppercorns
1 tablespoon chopped fresh lemon thyme (or regular thyme)
⅓ cup all-purpose flour
1 cup heavy cream

MAKES 4 SERVINGS

This is a classic recipe for New England clam chowder, which is still popular in Arthur Gordon Pym's hometown of Nantucket.

Drain the clams, reserving their juice, and rinse them under cold running water. Roughly chop the clams and place them in a small bowl with the juice of 1 lemon. Let the clams sit in the lemon juice for 1 hour in the refrigerator.

In a large saucepan over medium heat, cook the bacon to your desired doneness, and then transfer to a plate lined with paper towels to absorb the grease. Add the onion, celery, potatoes, and garlic to the bacon fat in the saucepan. Sauté just until the onions become translucent, about 5 minutes.

Add 1 cup water, 1 cup of the the reserved clam juice, vegetable broth, salt, pepper, and half of the thyme and stir to combine. Bring to a boil over medium-high heat, then decrease the heat and simmer for 10 minutes.

In a medium mixing bowl, use a whisk to combine the flour and cream. Slowly whisk the mixture into the soup until it is thoroughly combined. Bring to a boil, then decrease the heat and stir until thickened, 2 to 3 minutes. Add the clams and simmer for 1 minute longer, until the clams are heated through.

Fill each bowl with the clam chowder. Top each bowl with one-fourth of the bacon. Garnish with a sprinkle of pepper, the remaining thyme, and squeeze half a lemon over each bowl. Give each guest their own ration of homemade oyster crackers (page 56).

> **HIDEOUS HINT**
>
> *Create delicious and spooky faces on each bowl of chowder. Cut the unbaked cracker dough into circles for eyes and a mouth in your desired shape. Bake according to the directions in the recipe. The faces represent the despair and terrors that Arthur Gordon Pym faced.*

BEGUILING SALADS, SIDES, AND SOUPS

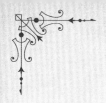

OYSTER CRACKERS

1 cup plus 2 tablespoons all-purpose flour

1 teaspoon baking powder

½ teaspoon sugar

½ teaspoon sea salt

2 tablespoons cold unsalted butter, cut into tiny squares

½ cup cold water, divided

Specialty Tool

Oyster cracker cutter (optional; can also cut out circles using a paring knife or very small cookie cutter)

This recipe is for the kind of classic oyster crackers that Arthur Gordon Pym might have carried along with him from his Nantucket home on his horrifying journey.

Preheat the oven to 350°F. Line a baking sheet with parchment paper.

In a large mixing bowl, add 1 cup of the flour, baking powder, sugar, and salt. Stir to combine.

Add the butter and ¼ cup cold water and use your fingertips to gently blend the cold pieces of butter into the ingredients. Ensure that all of the tiny chunks of butter get blended in. Use your hands to knead the dough for a few seconds. Add another ¼ cup of cold water to the dough and knead until the dough forms a ball. If too dry, add more water; if too sticky, add more flour.

Sprinkle the remaining 2 tablespoons flour on the countertop. Use a rolling pin to roll the dough out to about ½-inch thick. Press the oyster cracker cutter into the dough. Wiggle the cutter to make sure it has cut completely through the dough and the crackers can be easily removed.

Place the crackers on the prepared baking sheet and bake until the crackers are golden brown all around, 12 to 15 minutes. Remove from the oven and set on the countertop to cool.

Serve in small dishes for guests to add to chowders, soups, and stews or just to snack on a favorite New England cracker.

The grass wore the deep tint of the cypress, and the heads of its blades hung droopingly, and hither and thither among it were many small unsightly hillocks, low and narrow, and not very long, that had the aspect of graves, but were not; although over and all about them the rue and the rosemary clambered.

—"THE ISLAND OF THE FAY"

Island of the Fay ROSEMARY-SCENTED *Baked* STUFFED TOMATOES

1 tablespoon unsalted butter, softened

4 large vine-ripened tomatoes

1 cup breadcrumbs

¼ cup shredded mozzarella cheese

1 sprig fresh rosemary, leaves removed

¼ teaspoon sea salt

¼ teaspoon freshly ground multicolored peppercorns

4 sprigs fresh basil, to garnish

MAKES 4 SERVINGS

Poe wrote about rosemary in his 1841 short story "The Island of the Fay." At the time he wrote the story, fashionable restaurants had baked and stuffed tomatoes on their menus. The tomatoes in this recipe are just lightly scented by a sprig of rosemary.

Preheat the oven to 375°F. Grease a square baking dish or a pie pan with the butter.

Using a paring knife, cut a circle on the top of each tomato. Cut around the stem, cutting deep enough into the tomato to carve out a cavity to stuff, but not so deep that the knife cuts through the bottom of the tomato. Keep the cap of each tomato intact and set aside. Make a note of which tomato cap goes with which tomato! Turn the tomatoes upside down on a paper towel to drain.

In a medium bowl, combine the breadcrumbs, cheese, rosemary, salt, and pepper. Use a large spoon to fill the cavity of each of the tomatoes with the filling. Place the tops on the tomatoes and set the tomatoes in the prepared baking dish. Bake for 40 minutes, or until the breadcrumbs on top appear lightly toasted and the cheese is melted.

Garnish each with a sprig of basil.

BEGUILING SALADS, SIDES, AND SOUPS

Who does not remember that, at such a time as this, the eye, like a shattered mirror, multiplies the images of its sorrow, and sees in innumerable far-off places, the woe which is close at hand?

—"THE ASSIGNATION"

Shattered Mirror Soup: PEPPER-POT SOUP *with* MEATBALLS

Soup
- 2 tablespoons unsalted butter
- 1 tablespoon extra-virgin olive oil
- 1 red onion, chopped
- 2 medium potatoes, chopped
- 2 cloves garlic, minced
- 4 vine-ripened tomatoes, chopped
- 4 Scotch bonnet peppers, trimmed and seeded (can substitute any hot peppers)
- 4 cups vegetable stock
- 2 cups water
- ¼ cup chopped fresh cilantro
- 2 bay leaves
- Juice of 1 lemon
- 1 teaspoon pink Himalayan sea salt
- 1 teaspoon freshly ground peppercorns

Meatballs
- 8 ounces ground pork
- 8 ounces ground beef
- ½ cup whole milk
- 1 egg
- ½ cup crushed club crackers
- ½ cup diced red bell pepper
- ¼ cup chopped celery
- 1 tablespoon chopped fresh parsley, plus more for garnish
- ½ teaspoon each: minced garlic, minced shallot
- ¼ teaspoon each: ground allspice, ground nutmeg, mustard powder, pepper, salt
- Pimento-stuffed green olives

MAKES 4 SERVINGS

When Poe lived in Philadelphia, street vendors stood on corners crying out, announcing their wares. The "pepper-pot women" shouted: "Pepper-ee pot! All hot!" about their soup. This Pepper-Pot Soup recipe includes meatballs with olives for eyeballs. It also features Caribbean Scotch bonnet peppers, but any pepper with a bit of heat will work.

In a Dutch oven over medium-high heat, melt the butter and heat the olive oil. Add the onion, potatoes, garlic, and tomatoes. Sauté the vegetables for a few minutes, then add the peppers and stir to combine. After a few more minutes, add the vegetable stock and 2 cups water. Bring to a boil, and then decrease the heat to simmer. Add the cilantro, bay leaves, lemon juice, salt, and pepper. Simmer the soup for 30 minutes longer.

While the soup is simmering, preheat the oven to 375°F.

Line a baking sheet with parchment paper.

Place all of the meatball ingredients in a large mixing bowl. Using your hands, mix all of the ingredients together until they are just combined. Use a melon baller or ice-cream scoop to make 1-inch balls with the meat mixture. Roll each piece in your hands to make a smooth, round ball, about 4 balls in total. Place on the prepared baking sheet, 2 inches apart, and bake until golden brown and the meat reaches 160°F in the center, 20 to 25 minutes, or until edges are lightly browned all around.

Remove the meatballs from the oven and top each with an olive "eyeball." Serve on a platter for guests to add to their soup.

BEGUILING SALADS, SIDES, AND SOUPS

> *A* draught of this Médoc will defend us from the damps.
> —MONTRESOR, "THE CASK OF AMONTILLADO"

Chilled BLACKBERRY MÉDOC SOUP *with* FRESH MINT

2 cups fresh blackberries
½ cup Médoc wine
½ cup water
½ cup sugar
¼ teaspoon sea salt
¼ teaspoon freshly chopped ginger
6 sprigs fresh mint
2 cups plain yogurt
1 teaspoon fresh lemon juice
Optional: ¼ cup sour cream and House of Usher Party Crackers (page 23)

Eyeball garnish (optional)
4 canned lychees
4 large blueberries

MAKES 4 SERVINGS

In Poe's 1846 short story "The Cask of Amontillado," Montresor plots revenge on his nemesis by first getting him drunk on too much Médoc, a red wine, such as merlot or cabernet sauvignon, from the Médoc region in France.

In a large saucepan over medium heat, combine the berries, wine, ½ cup water, sugar, salt, ginger, and 2 sprigs of fresh mint. Bring to a boil, decrease the heat to medium-low, and simmer for 20 minutes. Remove from the heat and set on the countertop to cool. When cool, pour the mixture into a large bowl through a strainer, removing the seeds and mint.

Place the mixture in a blender, add the yogurt and lemon juice, and pulse until all of the ingredients are well blended.

Set the soup in the refrigerator to cool for at least 30 minutes. Pour the soup into bowls and garnish with the remaining 4 sprigs of fresh mint.

To make the eyeball garnish: Fill the inside of each of the lychees with a blueberry, and place in each bowl of soup.

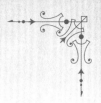

So that her highborn kinsmen came and bore her away from me, to shut her up in a sepulchre in this kingdom by the sea.

—"ANNABEL LEE"

Annabel Lee's CRAB BISQUE

¼ cup unsalted butter

1 teaspoon extra-virgin olive oil

1 teaspoon diced shallots

¼ cup all-purpose flour

½ teaspoon pink Himalayan sea salt

½ teaspoon freshly ground multicolored peppercorns

1½ cups vegetable stock

1½ cups whole milk

1½ cups heavy cream

8 ounces lump crabmeat

½ cup sherry

2 large lemons

Chopped fresh flat-leaf parsley, to garnish

Hot Hungarian paprika, to garnish

MAKES 4 SERVINGS

In his 1849 poem "Annabel Lee," the narrator and his love, Annabel Lee, presumably Poe's beloved wife, Virginia Clemm, enjoy their life together in a fictional "kingdom by the sea," which could very well be one of the cities on the mid-Atlantic Coast where Poe lived. This bisque, which was popular in Poe's New England, is made with sherry, which is a fortified wine that was prevalent when Poe wrote "Annabel Lee."

In a small saucepan over low heat, warm the milk. Set aside.

In a large saucepan over medium heat, melt the butter and heat the olive oil. Add the shallots and cook until translucent but not brown, 2 to 3 minutes. Add the flour, salt, pepper, and vegetable stock and whisk to combine. The whisk will help ensure the flour is completely dissolved and not lumpy. Add 1 cup of the warm milk and the cream. Whisk to combine.

Strain any liquid from the crabmeat, rinse under cold water, and add to the soup. Continue to cook for 5 to 7 minutes, stirring continuously, until the soup thickens. Add the sherry and remaining ½ cup warm milk and stir to combine. Squeeze the juice of 1 lemon and stir to combine.

Serve in soup bowls. Garnish with the parsley and paprika. Serve with a quarter of a fresh lemon for each guest to add as much as they like to their bisque.

HIDEOUS HINT

Optional: Create delicious and spooky faces for the top of each bowl of bisque. Cut frozen pastry dough into 3-by-2-inch rectangles. Use a paring knife to cut out circles to make two ghoulish eyes and a mouth. Line a baking sheet with parchment paper. Place the faces on the baking sheet and bake according to the directions on the pastry dough package.

BEGUILING SALADS, SIDES, AND SOUPS

Ghastly Delectable

MAIN COURSES

The "Red Death" had long devastated the country. No pestilence had been ever so fatal, or so hideous. Blood was its Avator and its seal—the redness and the horror of blood. There were sharp pains, and sudden dizziness, and then profuse bleedings at the pores, with dissolution.

—"THE MASQUE OF THE RED DEATH"

Prince Prospero's
ROASTED TURKEY DRUMSTICKS

Drumsticks
4 tablespoons extra-virgin olive oil
8 turkey drumsticks
½ teaspoon pink Himalayan sea salt
½ teaspoon freshly ground multicolored peppercorns

Cherry-Cranberry Compote
1 cup cherry jelly
1 cup canned cranberry sauce
¼ teaspoon lemon juice

Garnish
3 sprigs fresh sage
3 sprigs fresh rosemary

MAKES 8 SERVINGS

Like the turkey legs on Prince Prospero's medieval banquet table, these turkey legs are roasted until they are crisp and deep golden brown.

Preheat the oven to 375°F. Grease a Dutch oven or roasting pan with 2 tablespoons of the oil.

In a large skillet over medium heat, heat the remaining 2 tablespoons oil. Place the drumsticks in the skillet, sprinkle ¼ teaspoon each of salt and pepper over them, and brown them well on both sides, 8 to 10 minutes per side. Sprinkle the remaining salt and pepper on the bottom side after they are flipped. Place the cooked drumsticks in the prepared pan.

Roast the drumsticks in the oven, uncovered, until the internal temperature of the meat is 165°F, 1½ to 2 hours. Flip the drumsticks after the first 45 minutes; repeat after 30 minutes more.

To make the compote: In a medium saucepan over medium-high heat, combine the cherry jelly, cranberry sauce, and lemon juice. Bring to a bubble, and then decrease the heat to medium-low and cook for 2 minutes. Remove from the heat and set on the countertop.

Arrange the drumsticks on a large platter with a dish of the compote and garnish with the sage and rosemary.

> **HIDEOUS HINT**
>
> *Create blood spatter with red cake-decorating gel or compote juice.*

It was towards the close of the fifth or sixth month of his seclusion, and while the pestilence raged most furiously abroad, that the Prince Prospero entertained his thousand friends at a masked ball of the most unusual magnificence. It was a voluptuous scene that masquerade.

—"THE MASQUE OF THE RED DEATH"

Prince Prospero's BEEF WELLINGTON with PORT-WINE DUXELLES

2 cups sliced mushrooms
1 red onion, finely chopped
1 tablespoon chopped fresh thyme
2 tablespoons unsalted butter
2 tablespoons olive oil
½ teaspoon sea salt
¼ teaspoon freshly ground black pepper
1 cup port wine
One 2-pound beef tenderloin
3 tablespoons Dijon mustard
1 tablespoon whole-grain mustard
One 17.3-ounce package frozen puff pastry dough, thawed
3 ounces thinly sliced prosciutto
2 egg whites

Specialty Tool
6-inch masquerade mask cookie cutter (optional)

MAKES 4 SERVINGS

This beef Wellington is made with beef tenderloin and mushrooms simmered in port wine, which was a favorite of Poe's. The design on the pastry is a mask like the ones worn at Prince Prospero's masquerade party in Poe's story "Masque of the Red Death." Serve this with a side of port wine.

Preheat the oven to 400°F.

In a food processor, pulse the mushrooms, onions, and thyme until combined.

In a large skillet over medium heat, melt 1 tablespoon of butter and heat 1 tablespoon of the olive oil. Add the mushroom mixture and sauté until the onions are translucent, about 5 minutes. Add half of the salt and pepper. Add the wine and cook until it is evaporated. Remove from the skillet and place in a bowl. Season the beef with the remaining salt and pepper.

In the skillet over high heat, melt 1 tablespoon butter and heat the 1 tablespoon olive oil. Sear the beef until browned all around. Remove the beef from the skillet and spread the mustards around the beef.

Arrange 1 sheet of pastry dough on plastic. Place the prosciutto on the dough. Spread the mushrooms across the prosciutto. Place the beef on top, horizontally, and roll the dough around it, releasing the plastic as you roll. Tuck the dough together at ends to seal.

Using a mask-shaped cookie cutter, cut out the pastry dough and place the mask on top of the pastry casing. Cover the pastry dough with lightly beaten egg whites. Bake until golden brown and the middle of the beef reaches 120°F, about 45 minutes.

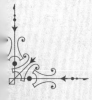

GHASTLY DELECTABLE MAIN COURSES

The islanders ... were among the most barbarous, subtle, and bloodthirsty wretches that ever contaminated the face of the globe.
—THE NARRATIVE OF ARTHUR GORDON PYM OF NANTUCKET

Barbarous Islanders' LOBSTER NEWBERG

8 ounces (1 sheet) frozen puff pastry dough
½ tablespoon butter
½ tablespoon extra-virgin olive oil
2 large shallots, diced
3 tablespoons tomato paste
1 tablespoon and ½ teaspoon hot Hungarian paprika, divided
½ teaspoon sea salt
⅓ cup dry red wine
1 cup vegetable stock
1 cup and 1 tablespoon heavy whipping cream
2 cups sliced mushrooms
1 pound lobster meat
2 tablespoons dry sherry
1 egg yolk
1 sprig fresh tarragon
3 sprigs fresh curly parsley
1 lemon, sliced

MAKES 2 LARGE OR 4 SMALL SERVINGS

This lobster Newberg celebrates the seafood culture of Arthur Gordon Pym's beloved Nantucket, as well as that of Poe's antebellum New England. The dish is made with sherry, which Poe was said to have loved. Sherry hails from Spain, where Poe's 1842 story "The Pit and the Pendulum" was set. Some of the best sherry is Amontillado sherry, which Poe celebrated in his 1846 short story "The Cask of Amontillado." Though potent, a shot of sherry is delicious served with this lobster Newberg.

Preheat the oven to 375°F.

Line a 9-by-12-inch baking sheet with parchment paper. Cut the pastry dough to a size that will fit a 9-inch-round pie plate. Place the dough on the baking sheet and bake until the pastry dough puffs up and is lightly browned, 15 to 20 minutes. When it is baked, remove the pastry and set it on the countertop.

In a large saucepan over medium heat, melt ¼ tablespoon of the butter and heat the oil. Add the shallots, tomato paste, paprika, and salt. Sauté until the shallots are translucent, 2 to 3 minutes. Add the wine. Bring to a boil, then reduce the heat and simmer slowly until the wine is evaporated, 10 to 15 minutes. Add the stock and 1 cup of cream. Bring to a boil, then reduce the heat to simmer for 15 minutes.

In a separate saucepan over medium heat, melt the remaining butter. Add the mushrooms and sauté for 15 minutes, stirring occasionally. Add the cream sauce, lobster meat, and sherry and simmer, stirring occasionally.

In a medium bowl, combine the egg yolk with the remaining cream and 1 tablespoon of the cream sauce. Whisk until thoroughly combined. Whisk into the lobster sauce in the other saucepan and simmer over low heat for 10 minutes, stirring occasionally.

Remove the pastry from the pie plate. Place the Newberg in the pie plate and top with the pastry. Garnish with fresh tarragon, parsley, and lemon slices arranged around the edge of the pie plate.

> **HIDEOUS HINT**
>
> *Use a paring knife to carve out eyes and mouth in the pastry dough to create a face of a barbarous islander.*

GHASTLY DELECTABLE MAIN COURSES 71

At the most remote end of the crypt there appeared another less spacious. Its walls had been lined with human remains, piled to the vault overhead, in the fashion of the great catacombs of Paris. Three sides of this interior crypt were still ornamented in this manner. From the fourth the bones had been thrown down, and lay promiscuously upon the earth . . .

—"THE CASK OF AMONTILLADO"

Catacombs ROASTED CAULIFLOWER

1 large head cauliflower

2 tablespoon extra-virgin olive oil

¼ teaspoon salt

¼ teaspoon freshly ground black peppercorns

6 small sweet peppers in multiple colors

6 vine-ripened tomatoes, on the vine

6 small red potatoes

2 shallots, peeled

1 large head garlic, with the top removed

6 red radishes, tops trimmed

1 small head radicchio (can substitute napa cabbage), cut into quarters

1 bunch fresh kale

MAKES 4 SERVINGS

This plant-based main course is inspired by the skulls that cover every inch of the catacombs in Poe's "The Cask of Amontillado." The "skull" is topped with a rich, flavorful, roasted red-pepper sauce. The gorgeous colors of the roasted radishes, beets, and peppers make a fantastic centerpiece that guests can pull apart and devour.

Preheat the oven 375°F. Line two baking sheets with parchment paper.

Trim the leaves and stem of the cauliflower, place on one of the prepared baking sheets, and drizzle the oil all over. Use your fingers to spread 1 tablespoon of the oil around the cauliflower to cover it well; sprinkle half of the salt and pepper over the top.

In a large mixing bowl, combine the peppers, tomatoes, potatoes, shallots, garlic, radishes, and radicchio. Add the remaining 1 tablespoon of oil, salt, and pepper, and use a large spoon to mix the ingredients so that the vegetables are coated evenly with the oil. Arrange the vegetables on the second prepared baking sheet. Roast both baking sheets until the vegetables are tender, 35 to 40 minutes, rotating the sheets midway through cooking.

Remove from the oven and set aside to cool. When the peppers are cool enough to handle, slit them open and remove the seeds and cores. Pulse four of the roasted red peppers in a food processor to create a sauce.

Arrange the kale leaves on a large serving platter. Place the roasted cauliflower in the center of the kale. Drizzle the sauce over the cauliflower. Arrange the other roasted vegetables around the cauliflower.

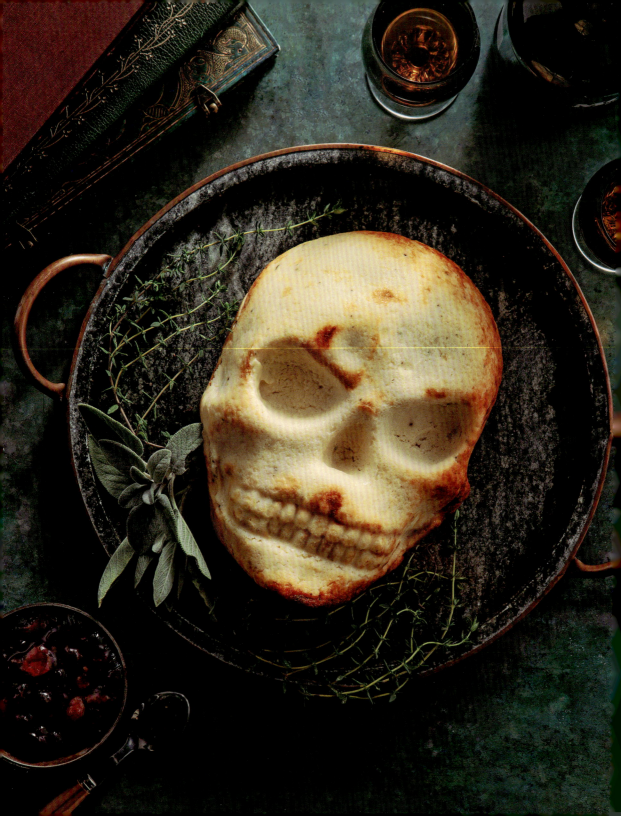

The New York Giants. Darkness and decay and the big blue hold dominion over all. The Baltimore Ravens. A thousand injuries they will suffer. Edgar Allan Poe evermore.

—THE POE TOASTER

TURKEY PUDDING *with* CHERRY-CRANBERRY COMPOTE

½ cup plus 1 teaspoon unsalted butter, softened

2 cups whole milk

4 eggs

½ cup all-purpose flour

¼ teaspoon ground mustard

¼ teaspoon sea salt

¼ teaspoon freshly ground black peppercorns

1 tablespoon cognac, plus enough to serve a shot to each guest with their meal

3 cups roasted turkey, cut into ½-inch squares

8 sprigs fresh thyme

6 sprigs fresh sage

MAKES 12 SERVINGS

In 2001, this message was left at Poe's resting place in Baltimore, Maryland, on his birthday, January 19. It was shortly before the Ravens and the Giants faced off in Superbowl XXXV.

For over half a century, someone (or possibly several people) have been seen visiting Poe's resting place on his birthday. The same man was purportedly seen for sixty years, sometimes raising a glass of brandy or whiskey. He became known as "The Poe Toaster."

Preheat the oven to 400°F. Grease a 9-inch round baking dish with 1 teaspoon of the butter.

In a large bowl, whisk the milk and eggs to combine. Set aside.

In a medium saucepan over medium heat, melt the remaining ½ cup butter. Whisk in the flour, ground mustard, salt, and pepper and cook for 2 to 3 minutes, until toasty. Add the milk and egg mixture and the cognac and whisk to combine. Place the mixture and the turkey in a blender with the leaves from 1 sprig of thyme. Pulse to blend all of the ingredients together well.

Transfer the mixture to the prepared baking dish and bake until a toothpick inserted into the center of the pudding comes out clean.

Remove from the oven and set on the countertop to cool slightly. Garnish with the remaining fresh thyme and sage. Serve with Cherry-Cranberry Compote (page 66) and a cordial glass full of cognac for each guest.

HIDEOUS HINT

Bake this in a silicone cake pan shaped like a skull and splatter traces of thinned-down Cherry-Cranberry Compote (page 66) over the skull. Place pimento-stuffed green olives in the eyes for a spookier effect.

GHASTLY DELECTABLE MAIN COURSES

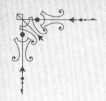

His eye was like the eye of a vulture.
—"THE TELL TALE HEART"

Vulture-Eye Pasta: SQUID INK PASTA *with Pan-Seared* SCALLOPS *and* RASPBERRY SAUCE

Lemon Compound Butter
½ cup unsalted butter, softened
¼ teaspoon fresh lemon juice

Scallops and Pasta
6 jumbo sea scallops
2 lemons
12 ounces squid ink pasta
1 teaspoon vegetable oil
¼ teaspoon freshly ground multicolored peppercorns
6 plump raspberries
6 sprigs fresh lemon thyme or thyme
2 sprigs fresh dill
1 lemon, cut into 6 slices

Specialty Tool
3½-by-3½-inch feather-shaped silicone chocolate mold

MAKES 6 SERVINGS

HIDEOUS HINT

For an extra spooky presentation, create bloody veins on top of the scallops with red cake-decorating gel.

Set on beds of squid ink pasta, these scallops resemble the hideous "vulture eyes" that Poe described in many of his writings. They are accented with tiny pieces of lemon compound butter molded into the shape of vulture feathers. A single raspberry gives them a bloodshot appearance.

To make the lemon compound butter: Place the butter and lemon juice in a food processor and pulse until combined. Press the butter mixture into feather-shaped molds. Cover with wax paper and set in the refrigerator for at least 1 hour, or overnight. Gently remove the butter from the molds when ready to plate the scallops.

To make the scallops and pasta: Place the scallops and the juice from 1 lemon in a bowl and toss lightly. Cover the bowl and set in the refrigerator to marinate.

Prepare the pasta according to the package directions.

In a medium saucepan over medium heat, heat the vegetable oil. Add the scallops, sprinkle with the pepper, and sauté until the scallops are lightly browned all around, 5 to 7 minutes on each side. Use tongs to carefully flip the scallops.

With a fork, twirl the pasta into a 1½-inch dome on a plate for each guest. Set a scallop on top of each dome of pasta. Place a raspberry on top of each. Garnish with the fresh herbs and lemon slices and arrange the butter vulture feathers randomly around the plates like they would fall naturally.

GHASTLY DELECTABLE MAIN COURSES

Quoth the raven nevermore.
—"THE RAVEN"

Raven's NESTS

These "raven" eggs are baked in little nests of lightly sautéed kale. Diced fresh red bell peppers add pops of color and flavor for a treat to satisfy the most ravenous appetite.

Grease the six springform pans with 1½ teaspoons of the oil. Place the springform pans on a baking sheet.

In a large saucepan over medium heat, heat the remaining 1½ teaspoons of olive oil. Add the kale and lightly sauté for 5 minutes. The kale will shrink down considerably. If there is not enough room in the saucepan for all the kale at the beginning, add the remaining kale when there is room. Add the salt and pepper and stir to combine.

Divide the kale among the springform pans, creating a nest in each pan. Add an egg to each nest. Sprinkle the red pepper, cheese, and some of the thyme on top of each nest and bake until the eggs are cooked through, 15 to 20 minutes.

Garnish with the remaining thyme and serve.

3 teaspoons extra-virgin olive oil

6 cups chopped kale

¼ teaspoon sea salt

¼ teaspoon freshly ground multicolored peppercorns

6 large eggs

1 large red bell pepper, cored, seeded, and diced

2 tablespoons grated Gouda cheese

8 sprigs fresh thyme

Specialty Tool
Six 4-inch round springform pans

MAKES 6 SERVINGS

GHASTLY DELECTABLE MAIN COURSES

Spirits moving musically, to a lute's well-tuned law . . .
—"THE HAUNTED PALACE"

GHOST PEPPER JELLY *and* CILANTRO CREAM CHEESE TEA SANDWICHES

8 ounces cream cheese, softened

¼ cup plus 1 teaspoon chopped cilantro

¼ teaspoon freshly squeezed lemon juice

¼ teaspoon salt

¼ teaspoon sugar

12 slices white bread

¼ cup ghost pepper jelly

MAKES 12 SERVINGS

When Poe arrived in New York City in April 1844 with his wife, Sissy, he wrote home to her mother about the fine tea and foods they were enjoying. Five years earlier, in his 1839 poem "The Haunted Palace," he wrote evocatively of a once-grand place in decline. Inspired by this eerie imagery, these lightly spicy tea sandwiches are made with ghost pepper jelly.

In a stand mixer or in a large bowl if using a handheld mixer, beat the cream cheese, ¼ cup of the cilantro, lemon juice, salt, and sugar on medium speed until well combined.

Use a knife to remove the crusts from the bread and cut each slice in half.

Spread the cream cheese mixture on half of the bread slices and top with a trace of the pepper jelly. Be very careful not to spread more than a very light amount because the jelly is exceedingly spicy. Top with the other half of the bread slices. Arrange the tea sandwiches on a platter and garnish with a sprinkle of the remaining cilantro.

The three of us—my two brothers and myself—had crossed over to the islands about two o'clock p.m., and had soon nearly loaded the smack with fine fish, which, we all remarked, were more plenty that day than we had ever known them.

—"A DESCENT INTO THE MAELSTROM"

Descent into the Maelstrom HASHED COD

1 pound cod or other white fish (fresh or frozen)

2 lemons

2 tablespoons chopped fresh dill

2 tablespoons chopped fresh parsley

2 tablespoons unsalted butter, softened

½ teaspoon hot Hungarian paprika

¼ teaspoon pink Himalayan sea salt

¼ teaspoon freshly ground multicolored peppercorns

8 ounces applewood-smoked or other bacon strips, cut into ½-inch pieces

12 small red potatoes, cut into ½-inch pieces

1 shallot, diced

1 red bell pepper, cored, seeded, and diced

MAKES 8 SERVINGS

Hashed fish was on menus at some of the nicest restaurants in New York City in the middle of the nineteenth century. As with corned beef hash, diced potatoes stretched a fine catch of fish or any meat, allowing it to last for multiple delicious meals. This recipe includes cod flavored with applewood-smoked bacon, as well as fresh dill and lemon juice.

About an hour before making the hash, place the fish in a bowl with the juice from one of the lemons. Slice the remaining lemon and set aside. Sprinkle with 1 tablespoon of the chopped dill. Cover the bowl and set it in the refrigerator.

Preheat the oven to 350°F. Grease a 9-inch round pie plate or baking dish with 1 tablespoon of the butter.

Remove the fish from the bowl and place in the prepared baking dish. Season with the paprika, salt, and pepper. Cut the remaining 1 tablespoon butter into small pieces and place on top of the fish. Bake until the fish flakes easily when tested with a fork, about 30 minutes.

While the fish is baking, prepare the hash. In a skillet over medium heat, cook the bacon for 7 minutes. Remove the skillet from the heat and use paper towels to absorb the bacon grease. Return the bacon to the skillet, and return the skillet to the heat. Add the potatoes and cook, undisturbed, for 3 to 5 minutes, then turn with a spatula to brown on all sides. Add the shallot and bell pepper and stir to combine. Sauté the hash until the shallots start to become translucent, about 15 minutes.

Remove the fish from the oven and use two forks to flake the fish into 1-inch pieces. Add the fish to the hash, stir to combine, and sauté for a few more minutes to marry the flavors. Garnish with the remaining dill and fresh parsley, and serve with the reserved lemon slices.

GHASTLY DELECTABLE MAIN COURSES

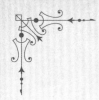

Open here I flung the shutter, when, with many a flirt and flutter, in there stepped a stately Raven of the saintly days of yore.

—"THE RAVEN"

Raven BLACK BEAN CAKES *with* CILANTRO CREMA

Black Bean Cakes

Two 15-ounce cans black beans, rinsed and drained

1 tablespoon jarred roasted red peppers, diced

1 teaspoon chopped shallot

1 small clove garlic, minced

¼ teaspoon sea salt

¼ teaspoon freshly ground peppercorns

Cilantro Crema

2 cups sour cream

¼ teaspoon fresh lime juice

¼ teaspoon sea salt

¼ teaspoon freshly ground multicolored peppercorns

2 tablespoons chopped fresh cilantro

Specialty Tool

6-by-2-inch silicone raven mold

MAKES 6 SERVINGS

These black bean cakes are shaped like a raven.

Preheat the oven to 350°F. Line a baking sheet with parchment paper.

In a food processor, pulse ¼ cup of the black beans into a paste to help hold the other ingredients and the remaining whole beans together. In a large bowl, combine the pulsed black beans, the remaining whole beans, red peppers, shallots, garlic, salt, and pepper. Use your hands to mix together well. Pack some of the mixture into the raven mold, then turn onto the prepared baking sheet. You may need to rework with your fingers in some spots to retain the raven shape. Repeat with the remaining mixture to make six cakes. Bake until firm and slightly browned, 20 minutes.

To make the cilantro crema: Combine the sour cream, lime juice, salt, pepper, and 1 tablespoon of the cilantro in a food processor and pulse until well combined. Serve with the black bean cakes, sprinkled with the remaining 1 tablespoon cilantro.

GHASTLY DELECTABLE MAIN COURSES

The arts keep you alive! They stimulate, encourage, challenge, and most of all, guarantee a future free of boredom. They allow growth and even demand it . . .

—VINCENT PRICE, DURING A TOUR OF THE POE HOUSE IN BALTIMORE, MARYLAND, IN MARCH 1978

Vincent Price's CHICKEN VERMOUTH with RICE

Chicken
4 chicken thighs and legs, skin on, about 3 pounds
½ teaspoon sea salt
½ teaspoon pepper
3 medium carrots, sliced
6 tablespoons diced celery
½ cup thinly sliced onion
1 clove garlic, minced
2 tablespoons chopped flat-leaf parsley
5 tablespoons dry vermouth
⅓ cup sour cream

Rice
1 cup long-grain white rice
1½ cups water
¼ teaspoon sea salt

MAKES 4 SERVINGS

Vincent Price may have starred in seven movies based on Edgar Allan Poe stories, but he was not the only family member to achieve fame. Vincent's grandfather invented an early version of baking powder, which he began selling commercially in 1863. Vincent was himself a gourmet cook. He starred in two cooking shows and wrote cookbooks: *A Treasury of Great Recipes* (1965) and *Come into the Kitchen* (1969). This an adapted recipe for Vincent Price's Chicken Vermouth with Rice.

Preheat the oven to 375°F.

Sprinkle the chicken with the salt and pepper. Place the chicken, carrots, celery, onion, garlic, parsley, and vermouth in a large casserole dish with a lid. Cover the dish with two thicknesses of foil and then place the lid on top of the foil. Bake for 1½ hours without removing the cover. The chicken should be at least 165°F in the center. When cooked, stir in the sour cream. For crispier, more browned chicken, remove the cover halfway through baking.

To make the rice: In a small saucepan over medium-high heat, combine the rice, water, and salt. Bring to a boil. Reduce heat to medium-low, and simmer until all water is absorbed. Remove from the stove and use a fork to lightly fluff the rice. Plate the 4 portions, serving the chicken and sauce over the rice.

HIDEOUS HINT

For a more potent punch of morose color and also nutrients, serve this over black rice.

GHASTLY DELECTABLE MAIN COURSES

Disolatrly Dilicious
DESSERTS

He told of a wild cry disturbing the silence of the night—of the gathering together of the household—of a search in the direction of the sound; and then his tones grew thrillingly distinct as he whispered me of a violated grave—of a disfigured body enshrouded, yet still breathing—still palpitating—still alive!

—"BERENICE"

Graveyard POKE CAKE

Cake
1 cup plus 2 tablespoons unsalted butter, softened
2 cups granulated sugar
4 eggs, at room temperature
3 cups all-purpose flour
1 tablespoon baking powder
1 cup milk, at room temperature
2 teaspoons vanilla extract
1½ cups raspberry or strawberry jam

This poke cake is decorated with miniature candy headstones and coffins; sour cream cookies in the shape of coffins and tombstones; edible flowers and herbs; mini chocolate skulls; meringue femur bones; and piles of crushed sandwich cookie "dirt." This cake is designed to portray the setting where the heroine was buried—alive—in Poe's 1835 short story "Berenice." Inside, red berry jam is added to places throughout the cake where long narrow holes are made with the end of a wooden spoon. When pieces of the cake are cut, the jelly-filled holes give the appearance of dripping blood.

To make the cake: Preheat the oven to 350°F. Grease a 9-by-13-inch cake pan with 2 tablespoons of the butter, making sure the bottom and sides are completely covered.

In a stand mixer or in a large bowl if using a handheld mixer, beat the remaining 1 cup butter and the granulated sugar on medium speed until the mixture becomes light and fluffy, 3 to 4 minutes. Add the eggs, one at a time, beating well after each addition.

In a separate medium bowl, stir together the flour and baking powder.

Add one-third of the flour mixture to the butter mixture, followed by one-third of the milk; repeat two more times until both are added to the butter mixture. After each addition, beat well, about 1 minute. Add the vanilla and beat to combine, about 1 minute.

Scrape the batter into the prepared pan and bake until the cake is browned on top and around the edges, it starts to pull away from the sides of the pan, and a toothpick inserted into the center comes out clean, 40 to 45 minutes. Remove from the oven and set on the countertop to cool for about 1 hour.

CONTINUES

DESOLATELY DELICIOUS DESSERTS

Chocolate Buttercream Frosting

6 cups powdered sugar

1 cup plus 1 tablespoon unsalted butter, softened

2 teaspoons vanilla extract

¼ cup milk

2 cups chocolate chips

Meringue Femur Bones, 15 to 18 bones, depending on size (Optional)

6 egg whites, room temperature

¼ teaspoon cream of tartar

¼ teaspoon salt

1 teaspoon vanilla extract

1½ cups granulated sugar

Decorations

3 cups chocolate sandwich cookie crumbs

3 ounces graveyard-theme cake-decorating sprinkles (tiny edible coffins, tombstones, femur bones, etc.)

5 Mini Chocolate Skulls (page 111)

5 Tombstone Cookies (page 110)

Specialty Tools

1½-round cake decorating tip

1 pastry bag for cake decorating

MAKES 12 SERVINGS

Use the end of a wooden spoon to poke 1-inch- and 2-inch-deep holes all around the cake.

Place the jam in a medium bowl and microwave for 45 seconds. Transfer to a piping bag fitted with a ¼-inch round decorating tip and pipe the jam into the holes.

To make the buttercream frosting: In a large mixing bowl, use a hand mixer to combine the powdered sugar, 1 cup of the butter, vanilla, and milk. Beat on high speed until thickened but still soft enough to work with using a piping bag, 8 to 10 minutes.

Place the chocolate chips and remaining 1 tablespoon butter in a microwave-safe bowl and microwave in 30-second increments, stirring in between, until melted and combined. Set the chocolate aside to cool. When the chocolate reaches room temperature, add it to the frosting. Stir well until there are no streaks. When the cake has cooled to room temperature, frost it with the buttercream frosting.

To make the meringue femur bones: Heat the oven to 225°F.

In the bowl of a stand mixer or in a large bowl if using a handheld mixer, beat the egg whites on low until they become foamy, 1 to 2 minutes. Add the cream of tartar, salt, and vanilla and increase the speed to medium until the eggs start to form soft peaks, 1 to 2 minutes.

Mixing on high, add the sugar slowly. Beat until stiff peaks form, about 5 minutes. Place the cake decorating tip in the pastry bag. Fill the pastry bag with the meringue. On a parchment-lined baking sheet, pipe a straight 2-inch line, and pipe 2¼-inch-round knobs at both ends. Repeat this until there are about 15 femur bones. Place the bones in the oven and bake until firm, about 90 minutes.

To decorate the cake: Decorate the cake with the meringue femur bones, sandwich cookie crumbs, sprinkles, mini chocolate skulls, and tombstone cookies.

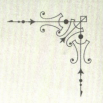

Not a speck on their surface—not a share on their enamel—not an indenture in their edges . . .
— "BERENICE"

Berenice's Teeth:
COOKIES and MARSHMALLOW DESSERT

4 large Tombstone Cookies (page 110)

2 cups vanilla buttercream frosting, homemade (page 99) or store-bought

50 mini marshmallows

8 sprigs fresh mint

MAKES 4 SERVINGS

In Poe's 1835 story "Berenice," a man fixates desperately on the last enduring vestige of his sickly and deteriorating betrothed, which is her teeth. He awakens from a trance to realize that after Berenice was inadvertently buried alive, he disturbed her grave and removed her teeth. The miniature marshmallows in this dessert resemble Berenice's gleaming, white teeth.

Cut the cookies in half. Spread the frosting on the bottom sides of each half of the cookie. Arrange the marshmallows on the frosting on the bottom cookie half. Place the top half cookie over the marshmallows. Garnish with fresh mint.

DESOLATELY DELICIOUS DESSERTS

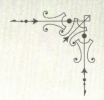

Tear up the planks! There! There! It is the beating of his hideous heart!
—"THE TELL-TALE HEART"

The Hideous Heart DESSERT

Gelatin Heart
1 tablespoon butter, for greasing the human heart mold

2 cups water, divided

12 ounces strawberry or raspberry gelatin powder

6 fresh raspberries

2 pounds red string licorice

Floorboards
One 7-ounce package ladyfinger cookies

1 cup chocolate buttercream frosting, homemade (page 88) or store-bought

1 tablespoon cocoa powder

16 sprigs fresh thyme

Cream
½ cup heavy whipping cream

1 teaspoon granulated sugar

½ teaspoon lemon juice

Specialty Tool
8-inch or 9-inch three-dimensional human heart–shaped plastic or silicone mold

MAKES 12 SERVINGS

In one of his most gruesome works, his 1843 short story "The Tell-Tale Heart," Poe describes a "hideous heart" that is still beating. This raspberry gelatin dessert is molded into the shape of a human heart, surrounded by twisted strings of red licorice veins.

To make the gelatin heart: Grease the inside of the mold with the butter.

In a small saucepan, boil 1 cup water. Add the gelatin powder and stir to dissolve. Add 1 cup cold water. Stir well to combine. Place the mold in a 9-inch-square baking dish and sturdy it with loose balls of aluminum foil. Place the berries in the mold, then pour the gelatin mixture in the mold. Let this set in the refrigerator for at least 4 hours or overnight.

Note: There will be more gelatin than the mold can hold. Dispose of extra gelatin or make a small bowl to serve on the side.

To make the floorboards: Layer frosting on one cookie, then top with another to create a cookie sandwich. Repeat until all the ladyfingers are used. Arrange the ladyfinger cookies alongside the gelatin like a pile of floorboards. Frost the cookies, and sprinkle with cocoa powder. Place thyme throughout.

To make the cream: In the bowl of a stand mixer or a large bowl if using a handmixer, beat the heavy whipping cream, sugar, and lemon juice together on low until well combined and starting to thicken so it won't splatter, 2 to 3 minutes. Increase the speed to high and beat the cream until thickened enough to form soft peaks, 12 to 15 minutes. Serve alongside the gelatin.

To assemble the dessert: Place the licorice on a large plate, creating a slight cavity where the gelatin heart will rest. Remove the gelatin heart from the mold by placing it upside down on the licorice and lifting the mold to release the gelatin. Serve with cream and lady finger cookies.

DESOLATELY DELICIOUS DESSERTS

*A*nd now was acknowledged the presence of the Red Death. He had come like a thief in the night. And one by one dropped the revelers in the blood-bedewed halls of their revel, and died each in the despairing posture of his fall. And the life of the ebony clock went out with that of the last of the gay. And the flames of the tripods expired. And darkness and decay and the Red Death held illimitable dominion over all.

—"THE MASQUE OF THE RED DEATH"

Prince Prospero's Uninvited Guest Cake: SPANISH BUN CAKE

2 tablespoons butter, softened
½ cup shortening
1 cup dark brown sugar
2 large egg yolks
2 cups all-purpose flour
¼ teaspoon freshly grated nutmeg
¼ teaspoon ground cinnamon
¼ teaspoon ground cardamom
½ teaspoon sea salt
1 vanilla bean pod
¾ cup whole milk

In Poe's 1842 short story "The Masque of the Red Death," an uninvited guest appears at midnight at Prince Prospero's exclusive masquerade party in his abbey. No one knows who is behind the mask. The group has been living in quarantine to avoid contracting the plague known as the Red Death. Spanish buns, or Spanish bun cakes, were popular when Poe wrote this story.

Preheat the oven to 350°F. Grease a 9 x 12-inch castle-shaped cake pan with 2 tablespoons of butter. In the bowl of a stand mixer or in a large mixing bowl if using a handheld mixer, cream the shortening and the brown sugar on medium speed. Beat in the egg yolks, one at a time, until both are combined well.

In a separate large mixing bowl, use your hands to mix the flour with the nutmeg, cinnamon, cardamom, and salt. Use a paring knife to open the vanilla bean pod and scrape the vanilla from inside. In another separate bowl, combine the milk and the vanilla.

Alternately combine the dry ingredients and the milk with the butter and shortening, beating on medium speed thoroughly after each addition.

Add the cake batter to the prepared castle-shaped cake pan and place in the oven. Bake until a toothpick comes out of the center clean.

CONTINUES

DESOLATELY DELICIOUS DESSERTS

Decorations

8 ladyfinger cookies

1 cup chocolate buttercream frosting, homemade (page 88) or store-bought

½ cup cocoa powder

4 fresh raspberries

8 sprigs fresh mint

6 sprigs fresh thyme

1 candy skull and skeleton

Specialty Tool

10-cup castle-shaped bundt cake pan

Nutmeg grater

MAKES 20 SERVINGS

When the cake is baked, remove it from the oven and set it on the countertop to cool. When it is cool, use a table knife to loosen the cake all around the edges of the cake pan. Place a cake platter on top of the bottom of the cake pan and use both hands to carefully turn the cake over and onto the cake platter.

Place the ladyfinger cookies in front of the door, like a pathway. Use a table knife to connect each cookie by spreading chocolate frosting between each of the cookies.

Sprinkle cocoa powder around the cake castle and the cookie pathway. Place a raspberry atop each turret of the castle. Arrange the fresh herbs all around to resemble Prince Prospero's abbey overgrown with vegetation, and place the candy skeleton nearby.

No rays from the holy Heaven come down on the long night-time of that town; but light from out the lurid sea streams up the turrets silently—gleams up the pinnacles far and free—up domes—up spires—up kingly halls—up fanes—up Babylon-like walls—up shadowy long-forgotten bowers of sculptured ivy and stone flowers—up many and many a marvelous shrine whose wreathed friezes intertwine the viol, the violet, and the vine.

—"THE CITY IN THE SEA"

The City in the Sea VIOLET ICE CREAM

5 large egg yolks
½ cup sugar
1 cup heavy whipping cream
1 cup whole milk
3 tablespoons crème de violette
Purple food coloring, as desired

Specialty Tool
Ice-cream machine (Optional; see recipe on page 97 for alternative ice cream preparation)

MAKES 16 SERVINGS

In his 1845 poem about a dying city that decays into the sea, Poe calls attention to the violets that grow on the doomed city's shrines. The story had a trajectory. Poe added the violets to his earlier versions of the poem, which were "The Doomed City" (1831) and "The City of Sin" (1836). This homemade ice cream gets its pretty light purple haze from crème de violette, a popular elixir during the Victorian era. The liqueur is made from violets steeped in brandy. A scoop of this ice cream will add an eye-catching pop of unusual color to a dessert. Serve it in an ice-cream parlor sundae glass or alongside a piece of Ligeia Dream Cake (page 106). Garnish with violet candies and fresh violets or pansies, which are edible flowers.

In a medium mixing bowl, whisk together the egg yolks and sugar until well combined.

In a medium saucepan over medium-high heat, add the cream and milk. Bring to a low boil, and then remove from heat. Slowly whisk the hot cream mixture into the egg mixture. Add the crème de violette and food coloring to achieve your desired shade and whisk to combine until there are no streaks of color.

Churn in an ice-cream maker according to the manufacturer's instructions.

CONTINUES

No-Churn ICE CREAM

3¼ cups heavy whipping cream

3 tablespoon sugar

One 14-ounce can sweetened condensed milk

2 tablespoons crème de violette

Purple food coloring, as desired

MAKES 16 SERVINGS

If you don't have an ice-cream machine, whip up an easy-to-make batch of no-churn ice cream.

Line a 9-x-12-inch cake pan with parchment paper.

In the bowl of a stand mixer or in a mixing bowl if using a handheld mixer, beat the cream and sugar on medium-high speed until the cream thickens, 5 to 6 minutes. Stir in the sweetened condensed milk, crème de violette, and food coloring to achieve your desired shade. Stir briefly for swirls of color or blend for 1 minute for a solid lavender color.

Scrape the mixture into the prepared pan and freeze for at least 12 hours, or until set.

DESOLATELY DELICIOUS DESSERTS 97

Nonsense! no!—the bug. It is of a brilliant gold color—about the size of a large hickory-nut—with two jet black spots near one extremity of the back, and another, somewhat longer, at the other. The antennae are—

—"THE GOLD-BUG"

William Legrand's Gold-Bug CAKE

Cake

Cooking spray

2 cups granulated sugar

½ cup plus 1 tablespoon unsalted butter, softened

½ cup vegetable oil

5 large eggs, separated into separate bowls of yolks and whites, at room temperature

2½ cups all-purpose flour

1 teaspoon baking powder

½ teaspoon baking soda

¼ teaspoon pink Himalayan sea salt

1 cup buttermilk

1 teaspoon vanilla extract

¼ cup canned coconut milk

¼ teaspoon cream of tartar

2 cups shredded coconut

When Poe wrote this story, coconut cakes were sold on street corners in Philadelphia each day by merchants known widely then as "cake men." Many of these Victorian street-food merchants were brought to the United States from Jamaica and the West Indies through the slave trade, and they made impacts on American culinary history with their food customs and traditions from their home countries. This cake depicts the brilliant bug in Poe's 1843 short story "The Gold-Bug." It is decorated with coconut covered in shimmering gold decorating spray and luster polish.

Preheat the oven to 350°F. Coat a dome-shaped cake pan with cooking spray. Sturdy the cake pan in a roasting pan. Twist pieces of aluminum foil to place around the cake pan to support it.

In the bowl of a stand mixer or in a large mixing bowl if using a handheld mixer, beat the granulated sugar, butter, and oil on medium-high speed until well combined. Add the egg yolks, one at a time, while continuously beating the mixture.

In a separate large mixing bowl, combine the flour, baking powder, baking soda, and salt.

Add the dry ingredients to the butter mixture, alternating if using the buttermilk, beating to combine well after each batch is added. Use a large spoon to stir in the vanilla and coconut milk.

In the bowl of a stand mixer or in a large mixing bowl if using a handheld mixer, beat the egg whites and cream of tartar on medium speed until peaks form when the beaters are lifted from the mixture. Use a large spoon to fold half of the egg whites into the cake batter, followed by the other half of the egg whites. Gently fold in 1 cup of the shredded coconut.

DESOLATELY DELICIOUS DESSERTS

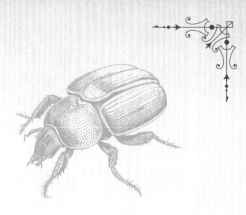

Vanilla Buttercream Frosting

6 cups powdered sugar

1 cup unsalted butter, softened

2 teaspoons vanilla extract

¼ cup milk

Decorations

One 1.5-ounce can gold decorating spray

8 ounces rolled black fondant

2 ounces rolled red fondant

One 1.5-ounce can cake-decorating glaze

4 cups fresh mint or other herbs

Specialty Tool

10-inch dome-shaped cake pan

MAKES 16 SERVINGS

Pour the cake batter into the prepared pan and bake until a toothpick inserted into the center comes out clean, 25 to 30 minutes.

To make the buttercream frosting: In a large mixing bowl using a handheld mixer, beat the powdered sugar, butter, vanilla, and milk on high speed until the frosting becomes thickened but is still soft enough to spread on the cake, about 4 to 5 minutes.

Cover a small table with clean cardboard and top the cardboard with two layers of parchment paper. Unmold the cake from the pan, place the cake in the center of the cardboard, and cover with the frosting. Sprinkle the remaining 1 cup of shredded coconut all around and on top of the frosted cake.

To decorate the cake: Spray the gold decorating spray all around the cake.

Use your fingers to form an 8-inch ball with the black fondant. Place the ball at the top of the cake for the head of the bug. Make two 1-inch balls with the red fondant. Press the palm of your hand gently on each round ball to flatten into ¼-inch disks for eyes and place the eyes on the head. Make eight ¼-inch balls with the remaining black fondant. Place two in the eyes for pupils and form six eyelashes and two antennae with the remaining balls. Place three eyelashes on top of each eye. Place the antennae at the top of the head. Divide the remaining black fondant into eight sections and roll out eight 10-inch-long legs. Place four legs on either side of the bug, radiating out from the center.

Spray the cake-decorating glaze all around the cake and fondant. Arrange the fresh mint around the cake to create something like the vegetation that William Legrand's gold-bug would have enjoyed on Sullivan's Island in South Carolina.

DESOLATELY DELICIOUS DESSERTS

"Fortunato!" No answer. I called again—"Fortunato!" No answer still. I thrust a torch through the remaining aperture and let it fall within. There came forth in return only a jingling of the bells. My heart grew sick—on account of the dampness of the catacombs. I hastened to make an end of my labor. I forced the last stone into its position; I plastered it up. Against the new masonry I re-erected the old rampart of bones. For the half of a century no mortal has disturbed them. In pace requiescat! (May he rest in peace.)

—"THE CASK OF AMONTILLADO"

The Cask of Amontillado DESSERT WALL

Cake
- 1½ cups plus 2 tablespoons unsalted butter, softened
- 4 ounces cream cheese, softened (half of a standard package)
- 1½ cup granulated sugar
- 1 vanilla bean pod
- 4 large eggs
- 2 cups all-purpose flour
- 1 teaspoon baking powder
- Pinch of salt

This cake depicts the grotesque scene in Poe's 1846 short story "The Cask of Amontillado" when Montresor buries Fortunato alive behind a wall in the catacombs. This wall is made with pound cake and covered with chocolate brick. Guests can use wooden mallets to break through the chocolate to tear down the wall. Behind the wall they will find another cake in the shape of a skeleton in a casket.

Preheat the oven to 350°F. Grease the loaf pan with 2 tablespoons of the butter.

In the bowl of a stand mixer or in a large bowl if using a handheld mixer, cream the remaining 1½ cups butter and the cream cheese on high speed for 1 to 2 minutes. Continue beating while slowly adding the sugar. Beat on high speed 1 to 2 minutes.

Use a paring knife to open the vanilla bean pod and scrape the insides into the bowl; beat for 1 minute longer. Decrease the speed to low and add the eggs, one at a time, beating after each addition. Add the flour, baking powder, and salt and mix on medium speed just until well combined.

Pour the cake batter into the loaf pan, set it in the oven, and bake until a toothpick inserted into the center comes out clean, 75 to 90 minutes.

Remove the cake and set on the countertop to cool for about 1 hour. When the cake is cool, turn it out of the loaf pan.

CONTINUES

Chocolate Wall
1 cup chocolate chips
1 tablespoon vegetable oil

Decorations
2 cups chocolate buttercream frosting, homemade (page 88) or store-bought
½ cup cocoa powder
Mini Chocolate Skulls (page 111), optional

Specialty Tools
1 standard loaf pan (8½ x 4½ x 2½ inches)
Bricks silicone onlay, 4 x 6¾ x ¼ inches
Pastry brush

MAKES 16 SERVINGS

To make the chocolate wall: In a large microwave-safe bowl, add the chocolate chips and vegetable oil and microwave in 30-second increments, stirring after each, until the chocolate is melted and combined.

Use a pastry brush to brush the chocolate onto the bricks silicone onlay, spreading the chocolate all across the silicone mold, to about ¼-inch thickness. Set in the refrigerator to harden for at least 1 hour. Clean the mold and repeat the process until you have enough bricks to surround the cake. Refrigerate all bricks for at least 1 hour before using.

To decorate: Use a table knife to frost the cake. Place the chocolate wall around the loaf cake. Arrange the mini chocolate skulls (see recipe on page 111) on top and around the cake. Very lightly sprinkle the cocoa powder around the cake.

I am by no means naturally nervous, and the very few glasses of Lafite which I had sipped served to embolden me no little, so that I felt nothing of trepidation, but merely uplifted my eyes with a leisurely movement, and looked carefully around the room for the intruder. I could not, however, perceive any one at all.

—"THE ANGEL OF THE ODD"

ARMAGNAC BRANDIED PEACHES

4 large or 8 small fresh peaches

Whipped cream (page 114)

2 cups Armagnac brandy, plus 6 ounces to serve a shot with each dessert

Specialty Tool
Cast-iron grill pan or grill

MAKES 4 SERVINGS

Lafite is a name of Armagnac, a brandy that hails from the Gascony region in southwest France. Just like the character in his 1844 short story "The Angel of the Odd," Poe loved brandy, and brandied peaches and other fruits were popular when he wrote this story. Serve these brandied peaches with freshly whipped cream and a side of Armagnac.

Use a paring knife to cut each peach in half and remove its pit. Place the peaches in a large mixing bowl and pour the brandy over them. Use a large spoon to drizzle the brandy, ensuring that each peach gets completely covered. Cover the bowl and refrigerate for at least 1 hour, or up to overnight.

Heat a grill pan over medium heat on the stovetop. When the grill is good and hot, place the peaches cut-side down and cook until they have grill marks, 1 to 2 minutes.

Arrange the peaches on a platter and serve with a dish of whipped cream and a shot of Armagnac brandy for each guest.

DESOLATELY DELICIOUS DESSERTS

And his eyes have all the seeming of a demon's that is dreaming, and the lamplight o'er him streaming throws his shadow on the floor; and my soul from out that shadow that lies floating on the floor shall be lifted—nevermore!

—"THE RAVEN"

Shadow CAKE

½ cup plus 1 tablespoon unsalted butter, softened

2 cups light brown sugar

2 eggs, separated

6 teaspoons cocoa powder

½ cup boiling water

1 teaspoon ground cinnamon

½ teaspoon freshly grated nutmeg

½ teaspoon ground ginger

2¼ cups all-purpose flour

1 teaspoon baking soda

½ teaspoon baking powder

½ teaspoon salt

½ cup buttermilk or milk with ½ teaspoon fresh lemon juice added and combined

1 vanilla bean pod

1 tablespoon powdered sugar

Specialty Tool

4-inch raven-shaped cookie cutter

MAKES 8 SERVINGS

This dark chocolate cake is a perfect backdrop for decorating in the theme of the shadows of Poe's best-known work, his 1845 poem "The Raven."

Preheat the oven to 350°F. Grease a 9-inch round cake pan with 1 tablespoon of the butter.

In the bowl of a stand mixer or in a large mixing bowl if using a handheld mixer, cream the remaining ½ cup butter and the light brown sugar on medium speed until light and fluffy, 6 to 7 minutes. Add the egg yolks and beat to combine.

In a separate mixing bowl, beat the egg whites until they become pillowy, about 2 minutes. In a separate small bowl, mix the cocoa with ½ cup boiling water until dissolved, then add the cocoa mixture to the egg whites along with the cinnamon, nutmeg, and ginger. Stir to combine.

In another mixing bowl, combine the flour, baking soda, baking powder, and salt. Add the dry ingredients to the butter mixture in three additions, alternating with the milk. Use a paring knife to cut the vanilla pod and scrape the seeds into the cake batter. Fold in the egg whites.

Pour the cake batter into the prepared cake pan and bake until a toothpick inserted into the center comes out clean, 35 to 40 minutes. Set the cake on a cooling rack.

Place a raven-shaped cookie cutter on a piece of parchment paper. Using a pen, trace the outline of the cookie cutter on the paper. Use scissors to carefully cut out the shape from the parchment paper. Tape the parchment paper to the top of the cookie cutter, ensuring that all edges are secured around the cutter with tape so that no powdered sugar sneaks through.

When the cake is cooled, set the cookie cutter in the center of the cake. Sprinkle powdered sugar generously around the cookie cutter, making sure that none of the powdered sugar gets inside the cookie cutter. Remove the cookie cutter to reveal the shape of a raven.

In beauty of face, no maiden ever equaled her. It was the radiance of an opium dream—an airy and spirit-lifting vision more wildly divine than the fantasies which hovered about the slumbering souls of the daughters of Delos.

—"LIGEIA"

Ligeia Dream Cake: POPPY-SEED CAKE *with* LEMON THYME

Cake
1 cup butter, plus more for greasing the pan, softened
2½ cups all-purpose flour
1 teaspoon salt
½ teaspoon baking powder
½ teaspoon baking soda
1½ cups granulated sugar
2 eggs
3 egg yolks
1½ teaspoons vanilla extract
1 cup milk
2 tablespoons poppy seeds
1 tablespoon fresh lemon thyme leaves, plus extra for garnish

Frosting
1½ cups powdered sugar
½ cup unsalted butter, softened
½ teaspoon vanilla extract
¼ cup milk

Specialty Tools
10-inch, dome-shaped cake pan

MAKES 16 SERVINGS

The seed pods of poppies contain opium, to which Poe referred in his 1838 short story "Ligeia." This lighter variation of classic lemon poppy-seed cake is not overpowering in lemon flavor. It gets a subtle hint of lemon from fresh lemon thyme. The cake is topped with a light, thinned-down powdered sugar frosting, fresh thyme, and a sprinkle of poppy seeds. Serve a piece of cake to each guest with a big scoop of The City in the Sea Violet Ice Cream (page 95).

Preheat the oven to 375°F. Grease a 9-inch round cake pan.

In a large mixing bowl, whisk together the flour, salt, baking powder, and baking soda.

Using an electric stand mixer or a handheld electric mixer, cream the butter and granulated sugar on medium-high speed until light and airy, 5 to 6 minutes. With the mixer on low speed, beat in the eggs and egg yolks, one at a time. Continue beating and gradually add vanilla. Combine all ingredients well. Mix in half of the flour mixture; add half of the milk, followed by the remainder of the flour mixture. Add the remainder of the milk. Mix on high speed for 25 to 30 seconds.

Using a wooden spoon or spatula, fold about one-fourth of the poppy seeds and the lemon thyme leaves into the cake batter.

Scrape the batter into the prepared pan and bake until a toothpick inserted into the center comes out clean, 35 to 40 minutes. Set the cake aside to cool, then turn out of the pan onto a serving platter.

To make the frosting: In a large mixing bowl, mix all of the ingredients together. Add more milk to achieve a thinner frosting.

Frost the cooled cake and sprinkle with remaining poppy seeds. Garnish with fresh lemon thyme in the center and on serving plates.

DESOLATELY DELICIOUS DESSERTS

She was buried—not in a vault, but in an ordinary grave in the village of her nativity.
—"THE PREMATURE BURIAL"

Lafourcade Family Graveyard TRIFLE

1 recipe Prince Prospero's Uninvited Guest Cake (page 92), cut into squares

1 recipe Apple Compote (page 110)

1 recipe Vanilla Pudding (page 111)

2 cups heavy whipping cream beaten with 1 tablespoon sugar

One 13.3-ounce package chocolate sandwich cookies, crushed into crumbs

1 recipe Tombstone Cookies (page 110)

4 Mini Chocolate Skulls (page 111)

Gummy worms

Sprigs fresh thyme and other herbs

Specialty Tool

8½-inch-wide-by-7¾-inch-high clear glass trifle bowl

MAKES 16 SERVINGS

This classic trifle is full of warm notes of lightly spiced autumn flavors. It is an eye-catching centerpiece of voluptuous sweet treats, that, at a closer look, reveals signs of the graveyard where Mademoiselle Victorine Lafourcade was buried alive in Poe's 1844 short story "The Premature Burial." Squirmy gummy worms seem to slither through the layers of freshly whipped cream, cake, cinnamon-y apple compote, vanilla pudding, and crushed chocolate sandwich cookies. The top is decorated with sour cream cookies cut in the shape of tombstones. Mini chocolate skulls stick up through the cream and cookie topping. Put your guests to work as gravediggers, giving them each their own tiny shovel to dig into these flavorful layers.

Place half of the cake squares on the bottom of the trifle bowl. Spread half of the apple compote across the layer of cake. Spread half of the pudding across the compote. Spread half of the cream across the pudding. Repeat the layers, and then top with crushed cookies. Decorate the top with the tombstone cookies, mini chocolate skulls, and gummy worms. Arrange fresh thyme and other herbs to give the appearance of an overgrown cemetery.

DESOLATELY DELICIOUS DESSERTS

TOMBSTONE COOKIES

4 cups all-purpose flour, plus more for dusting
1 teaspoon baking soda
1 teaspoon baking powder
1½ teaspoons salt
1½ cups sugar
1 cup butter-flavored shortening or regular shortening
1 cup sour cream
2 large eggs
1 teaspoon vanilla extract

Specialty Tool
Coffin- and tombstone-shaped cookie cutters

MAKES 24 COOKIES

In a large mixing bowl, whisk together the flour, baking soda, baking powder, and salt.

In a stand mixer or another mixing bowl if using a handheld mixer, beat the sugar, shortening, sour cream, eggs, and vanilla on medium-high speed. Add the flour mixture and beat to combine. Cover the cookie dough with plastic wrap and chill in the refrigerator for at least 1 hour.

Preheat the oven to 350°F. Line a baking sheet with parchment paper.

Remove the dough from the refrigerator. Sprinkle a light dusting of flour on the countertop. Use a rolling pin to roll the dough to ¼-inch thick. The dough should not stick to your hands. Add flour as needed if the dough is sticky. Use cookie cutters to cut shapes out of the dough and place on the prepared baking sheet.

Bake until the cookies are lightly browned all around, 10 to 15 minutes. Remove from the oven and set on the countertop to cool.

There will be enough dough to make more cookies than are needed for the trifle. Use the remaining dough to cut out cookies in the shape of skulls, bones, ravens, cats, and other shapes to serve with the trifle.

APPLE COMPOTE

1 vanilla bean pod
5 large Honeycrisp apples, peeled, cored, and cut into 1-inch pieces
Juice of ½ lemon
½ cup brown sugar
½ cup water
1 cinnamon stick
¼ teaspoon ground nutmeg
¼ teaspoon ground ginger
¼ teaspoon ground allspice

MAKES 4 TO 6 SERVINGS

Use a paring knife to open the vanilla bean pod and scrape out the seeds.

Add all of the ingredients to a medium saucepan over medium-high heat. Bring to a boil, stirring. Decrease the heat to medium and cook until the apples are tender, 35 to 40 minutes. Remove the apple compote from the heat and set aside to cool on the countertop. Remove the cinnamon stick before serving.

VANILLA PUDDING

3 tablespoons cornstarch
3 cups whole milk
1 cup sugar
¼ teaspoon pink Himalayan sea salt
3 egg yolks
1 vanilla bean pod or ¼ teaspoon vanilla extract
1 tablespoon unsalted butter, softened

MAKES 4 TO 6 SERVINGS

In a large mixing bowl, whisk the cornstarch with ¼ cup of the milk.

In a medium saucepan over medium heat, whisk together the remaining 2¾ cups milk, sugar, and salt. Cook, stirring occasionally, until steam rises.

In a medium bowl, whisk the egg yolks. Pour ½ cup of the steaming milk into the egg yolks and stir continuously. Slowly pour the egg mixture and the cornstarch mixture into the saucepan and simmer, whisking continuously, until the mixture thickens, about 2 to 3 minutes. Remove from the heat.

Using a paring knife, open the vanilla bean pod and scrape the seeds into the pudding. Stir in the butter. Place a layer of plastic wrap directly on the top to prevent a skin from forming. Let cool in the refrigerator.

MINI CHOCOLATE SKULLS

3 teaspoons coconut oil
2 cups chocolate chips (or white chocolate chips)
Cooking spray

Specialty Tool
1 sheet mini skull-shaped candy molds, 6¼ x 4¾ x ¾ inches

MAKES 48 MINI CHOCOLATE SKULLS

In a double boiler over medium-low heat, or in a microwave-safe bowl in the microwave, place the oil and chocolate. Use a whisk to stir until well combined. If using the microwave, microwave for 1 minute, whisking after 30 seconds. Ensure the chocolate is smooth and all the lumps are dissolved.

Lightly spray cooking spray inside the skull molds. Wipe away excess with a soft cloth.

Use a small spoon to place chocolate into each of the skull molds. Ensure that each of the molds is filled completely. Lay a piece of wax paper over the molds, and place in the refrigerator until the chocolate is firm enough to remove from the molds without breaking, about 4 hours.

Once set, carefully pull the chocolate from the molds. If chocolates are not coming out, quickly dip the tray into a pan of hot water for 1 to 2 seconds.

DESOLATELY DELICIOUS DESSERTS

Pies all hot! meat and fruit, pies all hot!

—"THE CRY OF THE PENNY PIE MEN," AS DESCRIBED BY HENRY MAYHEW IN A LETTER TO THE MORNING CHRONICLE, DECEMBER 4, 1849

The Penny Pie Man's PIES

Poe's six years in Philadelphia were some of his most creative and productive. While he lived there, street vendors known as "penny pie men" sold savory and fruit-filled hand pies on the street corners. This assortment of pies can be made as hand pies like the penny pie men sold but here we use a 9-inch round store-bought frozen pie crust. Use a fork to poke air holes in the bottom and sides of the crust. Prebake the empty crust in a 350°F oven for 10 minutes, and then remove from the oven. Then add one of the pie fillings below and continue to bake until the crust is golden brown on the edges and the pie filling is firmly set (see the individual recipes for baking times). The pies are best with a spoonful of freshly whipped cream (page 114).

LEMON PIE

1½ cups sugar
¼ cup cornstarch
1½ cups water
4 egg yolks
2 tablespoons lemon juice
Zest from 2 large lemons
2 tablespoons unsalted butter

MAKES 8 SERVINGS

Some consider the lemon pies that were sold in the 1840s in Philadelphia at confectionary shops like Goodfellow & Coates, 71 South Sixth Street, the predecessors to today's lemon meringue pie.

Preheat the oven to 350°F. Prebake the pie crust (see headnote).

In a medium saucepan over medium heat, whisk together the sugar, cornstarch, 1½ cups water, egg yolks, lemon juice, and lemon zest. Cook, whisking, for 10 to 15 minutes until the pie filling thickens. Remove from the heat and stir in the butter. Pour the filling into a prebaked crust and bake until the crust is lightly browned around the edges and the filling is firmly set and not jiggly, 40 to 45 minutes. Remove from the oven and set on the countertop to cool.

VINEGAR PIE

1 vanilla bean pod
1⅓ cups sugar
4 eggs, at room temperature
1 tablespoon apple cider vinegar or fire cider
¼ cup unsalted butter, melted

MAKES 8 SERVINGS

Vinegar pie doesn't taste like vinegar. It contains only a trace of vinegar and is actually a very custard-forward dessert. Make this recipe with apple cider vinegar or, if available, a spot of fire cider.

Preheat the oven to 350°F. Prebake the pie crust (see headnote).

Use a paring knife to open the vanilla bean pod and scrape out the seeds. Add to a large mixing bowl with the remaining ingredients and whisk to combine. Pour into a prebaked pie crust and bake until the edges of the pie crust and the top of the pie are golden brown, and the filling is firmly set, 35 to 40 minutes. When the pie is cooked, it should be a little jiggly, but mostly firm. Remove from the oven and set on the countertop to cool for 5 minutes. While this pie can be eaten when cooled, it is best when it has been placed in the refrigerator to cool for 1 hour or longer.

FUNERAL PIE

1 cup golden raisins
⅔ cup sugar
2½ tablespoons cornstarch
¼ teaspoon sea salt
¼ teaspoon ground ginger
¼ teaspoon freshly grated nutmeg
¼ teaspoon ground cardamom
¼ teaspoon ground cinnamon
½ cup whole milk
⅔ cup sour cream
3 egg yolks

MAKES 8 SERVINGS

This is a variation of a popular dessert that was made for funerals in the Victorian era. Known as "funeral pies," these pies were made with raisins and sour cream.

Preheat the oven to 350°F. Prebake the pie crust (see headnote).

In a large saucepan over medium heat, cover the raisins with water and bring to a boil. Remove from the heat and set on the countertop to cool.

In a separate saucepan over medium-high heat, add the sugar, cornstarch, salt, ginger, nutmeg, cardamom, and cinnamon and whisk to combine. Add the milk and sour cream, whisking until the pie filling is a smooth consistency. Continue to whisk until the pie filling thickens, about 3 to 5 minutes. Decrease the heat to medium-low, add the egg yolks, and bring to a boil, whisking constantly. Boil for 1 minute. Remove from the heat and set on the countertop.

Strain the liquid from the raisins and add the raisins to the pie filling. Pour into the prebaked pie crust and bake until filling firms, about 15 minutes. Remove from the oven and set on the countertop to cool. While this pie can be eaten when cooled, it is best when it has been placed in the refrigerator to cool for 1 hour or longer.

DESOLATELY DELICIOUS DESSERTS

*Thou wast that all to me, love, for which my soul did pine—
a green isle in the sea, love, a fountain and a shrine, all wreathed
with fairy fruits and flowers, and all the flowers were mine.*

—"TO ONE IN PARADISE"

Paradise Pears: MOLASSES-POACHED PEARS *with* PORT WINE

Pears
4 large Anjou or Bosc pears, stems intact
1 cup port wine
2 cups water
½ cup molasses
Juice of 1 lemon
2 tablespoons honey
1½ teaspoons ground cinnamon, plus more for sprinkling
1½ teaspoons ground nutmeg, plus more for sprinkling
2 star anise
2 cinnamon sticks
1 vanilla bean pod

Whipped Cream
2 cups heavy whipping cream
½ cup sugar
½ teaspoon fresh lemon juice
4 large mint leaves

MAKES 4 SERVINGS

Seasonal fruit—pears—star in this recipe for one of the Victorian street food treats that were popular when Poe wrote his 1834 poem "To One in Paradise." Throughout New York and Philadelphia, Poe would have heard vendors, on foot, crying out, "Molasses pears! Come and get your molasses pears!"

Use a paring knife to peel the pears, carefully removing just the skin and retaining the shape of each pear. Leave the stems intact.

In a large saucepan over medium-high heat, combine the wine, 2 cups water, molasses, lemon juice, honey, cinnamon, nutmeg, star anise, and cinnamon sticks. Use a paring knife to open the vanilla bean pod and scrape the seeds into the pan. Stir to combine. Add the pears and simmer over medium heat until they achieve an amber color and fork-tender consistency, about 30 minutes. Turn the pears after 15 minutes to ensure an even color all around.

To make the whipped cream: Using a stand mixer or in a bowl if using a handheld mixer, beat the cream, sugar, and lemon juice on high speed until thickened, 10 minutes. Start on slow speed and increase the speed as the cream thickens.

Stand a poached pear on each serving plate and place a spoonful of cream alongside. Place a mint leaf where the pear leaf would be. On top of each pear, drizzle a bit of the poaching liquid and sprinkle a few shakes of ground cinnamon and nutmeg.

> **HIDEOUS HINT**
>
> *Serve these warm pears with a ghoulish cookie tucked into the cream (see Tombstone Cookies, page 110).*

DESOLATELY DELICIOUS DESSERTS

I continued, as was my wont, to smile in his face, and he did not perceive that my smile now was at the thought of his immolation.

—"THE CASK OF AMONTILLADO"

Cask of Amontillado CANNOLI

Poe's 1846 short story "The Cask of Amontillado" was set in Italy during the pre-Lenten Carnevale season. This recipe for cannoli, a classic Italian Carnevale treat that is loved around the world, represents the setting of what is arguably one of Poe's most gripping and gruesome stories.

Shells
- 2 cups all-purpose flour
- 1 tablespoon granulated sugar
- ¼ teaspoon pink Himalayan sea salt
- ¼ teaspoon ground cinnamon
- 2½ tablespoons cold unsalted butter, cut into tiny pieces
- ½ cup dry marsala wine or another dry white wine
- 1 large egg yolk, slightly beaten
- Zest of ½ lemon
- Vegetable oil, for frying

Filling
- 2 cups ricotta cheese
- 1 cup powdered sugar
- ½ teaspoon vanilla extract
- Zest of ½ lemon

Decorations
- 2 tablespoons coarsely chopped pistachios
- 2 tablespoons semisweet chocolate chips, coarsely chopped
- 1 tablespoon powdered sugar

Specialty Tools
- 4-inch round cookie cutter
- Set of 6 mini stainless-steel cannoli forms
- Piping bag with a ¼-inch round tip

MAKES 6 SERVINGS

To make the shells: In large mixing bowl, whisk together the flour, granulated sugar, salt, and cinnamon. Add the butter and use your fingers to blend the butter into the dry ingredients. Add the wine, egg yolk, and lemon zest, and stir until just combined. Do not knead the dough. Form the dough into a ball, wrap in plastic wrap, and set it in the refrigerator for 1 hour.

Divide the dough into six even pieces. The dough will be flaky. On a lightly floured surface, roll out each piece to a ¼-inch thickness. Use a 4-inch round cookie cutter to cut out each cannoli. Wrap a circle of dough around each of the cannoli forms, ensuring there is plenty of overlap to connect the two sides. Use your fingers to gently press down on the dough where it overlaps.

Pour the vegetable oil into a Dutch oven to a depth of 3 inches. Over medium-high heat, heat the oil. When the oil reaches 350° to 360°F, use tongs to delicately place each of the shells into the hot oil to fry. The shells will finish fast and can burn. Watch the thermometer carefully to ensure the shells are not in oil hotter than 360°F. Decrease the heat if necessary to keep the temperature at 360°F. Use tongs to turn the shells so they brown evenly, about 2 minutes. Remove from the oil and set on paper towels on a large plate. While the shells are still warm, use tongs to carefully wiggle the forms out of the shells.

To make the filling: Place the ricotta in a strainer to strain any excess liquid. In a large bowl, add the strained ricotta, powdered sugar, vanilla extract, and lemon zest and stir to combine. Place the filling in a piping bag with a ¼-inch round tip. When the shells have cooled, pipe the filling into each side of the shells.

To decorate the cannoli: Dip the end of each cannoli, where the cheese mixture is exposed, into either the chopped pistachios or the chopped chocolate chips. Sprinkle with powdered sugar.

DESOLATELY DELICIOUS DESSERTS

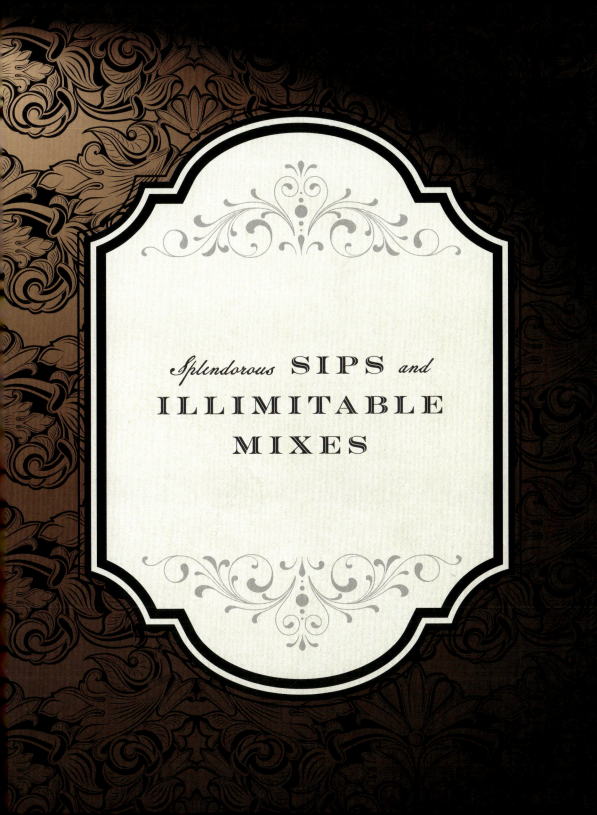

Splendorous SIPS *and* ILLIMITABLE MIXES

The prince had provided all the appliances of pleasure. There were buffoons, there were improvisatori, there were ballet dancers, there were musicians, there were cards, there was beauty, there was wine. All these and security were within. Without was the "Red Death."

—"THE MASQUE OF THE RED DEATH"

Prince Prospero's Angel of the Odd KIRSCH MULLED WINE with CHOKEBERRIES

One 750 ml bottle dry red wine
2 ounces Kirsch
1 teaspoon chokeberries
½ teaspoon juniper berries
¼ teaspoon whole cloves
3 star anise
1 vanilla bean pod, split and scraped
2 cinnamon sticks
1 orange, ½ cut into 4 slices, the other half for juice
1 lemon, ½ cut into 2 slices, the other half for juice

MAKES 6 SERVINGS

In his 1842 short story "The Masque of the Red Death," Poe writes about the wine Prince Prospero supplied to those who huddled away with him in his abbey while the plague ran rampant outside. Grogs (rum hot toddies), mead, wassail, and mulled wines were staples in the medieval era when the story takes place. This mulled wine is spiked with flavorful Kirschwasser, or cherry liqueur, which Poe wrote about in his 1844 short story "The Angel of the Odd." Poe wrote: "Hereupon, the Angel of the Odd replenished my goblet (which was about a third full of Port) with a colorless fluid that he poured from one of his hand bottles. I observed that these bottles had labels about their necks, and that these labels were inscribed 'Kirschwasser.'"

In a large saucepan over medium-high heat, combine all of the ingredients and bring to a boil. Lower the heat to medium and simmer for 20 to 23 minutes. Strain through a strainer into mugs. Garnish with small slices of fruit.

HIDEOUS HINT

Poe wrote that one of the symptoms of the Red Death was blood leaking through the victim's pores. Use red cake-decorating gel to make blood drips around the rims of the glasses.

SPLENDOROUS SIPS AND ILLIMITABLE MIXES

> "Drink," he said, "to the buried that repose around us. And I to your long life."
> —"THE CASK OF AMONTILLADO"

Poe Family EGGNOG

15 eggs, separated
2 cups sugar
A fifth (750ml) of brandy of
4 ounces Jamaican rum
1 pint heavy whipping cream, whipped
4 ounces heavy cream
Ground nutmeg, for sprinkling

MAKES 16 SERVINGS

In the book *A Second Helping of Murder* (2001), Anne Poe Lehr, a cousin of Edgar Allan Poe, shared what she believed to be the Poe family recipe for eggnog. Anne wrote: "It is delicious, booze-laden, and guaranteed to clog all arteries. The brandy 'cooks' the eggs while the eggnog pickles the drinker." She said that the recipe was tucked in a secretary that the Poe family owned since at least 1790. John and Frances Allan of Richmond, Virginia, took in Edgar Allan Poe as an infant after his mother passed away, which makes it challenging to determine whether Edgar Allan Poe ever actually knew this recipe. However, it certainly represents recipes of his time.

In a large mixing bowl, beat the egg yolks and gradually add the sugar. Continue beating until stiff. Very slowly add the brandy and rum to the yolk and sugar mixture. Add the whipped cream and heavy cream; stir.

In a separate mixing bowl, beat the egg whites until soft and pillowy, about 5 minutes. Fold the beaten egg whites into the egg-yolk mixture, cover the bowl with plastic wrap, and chill in the refrigerator until cold. Pour into serving glasses and sprinkle with ground nutmeg.

SPLENDOROUS SIPS AND ILLIMITABLE MIXES

Keeping time, time, time, in a sort of runic rhyme, to the tintinnabulation that so musically wells from the bells, bells, bells, bells, bells, bells, bells— from the jingling and the tinkling of the bells.

—"THE BELLS"

Tintinnabulation TEA BLEND

1 teaspoon black tea
1 teaspoon butterfly pea-flower tea
1 star anise
Thin lemon peels, to garnish

Specialty Tool
1 empty tea bag or tea infuser

MAKES 1 SERVING

In Poe's 1849 poem "The Bells" he refers to the tintinnabulation of the ringing bells. This dark and tranquil tea would be perfect on an icy night like the one Poe describes in this happy, merry poem.

Combine the teas in a tea bag or infuser and steep in hot water in a teacup with the star anise. Garnish with the lemon peel.

SPLENDOROUS SIPS AND ILLIMITABLE MIXES

> "I could have clasped the red walls to my bosom as a garment of eternal peace. "Death," I said, "any death but that of the pit!" Fool! might I have not known that into the pit it was the object of the burning iron to urge me?"
>
> —"THE PIT AND THE PENDULUM"

The Pit and the Pendulum
SPANISH COFFEE

1 orange slice

1 tablespoon cinnamon sugar

4 ounces freshly brewed coffee

2½ ounces ounces coffee liqueur

1 ounce Cointreau

½ ounce brandy

2 ounces freshly whipped cream

1 cinnamon stick

MAKES 1 SERVING

Poe's 1842 short story "The Pit and the Pendulum" is set in Spain during the Spanish Inquisition (1478–1834). Although Spanish coffee as it is known today is a modern invention (1970s), this is a perfect, warming cocktail for curling up with one of Poe's most hair-raising stories.

Wet the rim of a coffee mug by running an orange slice around it. Spread the cinnamon sugar on a plate and dip the rim of the mug in the cinnamon sugar. Pour in the hot coffee, coffee liqueur, Cointreau, and brandy. Top with the whipped cream. Garnish with the cinnamon stick.

> **HIDEOUS HINT**
>
> *Splatter a tiny drop of cherry juice across the froth of this coffee to suggest blood. Serve with a pendulum-shaped cookie.*

SPLENDOROUS SIPS AND ILLIMITABLE MIXES

> *I live continually in a reverie of the future.*
> —EDGAR ALLAN POE, IN A LETTER WRITTEN JULY 2, 1844

The Time Traveler:
SAZERAC with LEMON-THYME ICE

Lemon-Thyme Ice
3 sprigs lemon thyme

Cocktail
1½ ounces whiskey
¼ ounce absinthe
1 miniature pansy flower
1-inch piece lemon peel

Specialty Tool
Extra-large 3D skull ice-cube mold (optional)

MAKES 1 SERVING

Poe's 1848 prose poem "Eureka: An Essay on the Material and Spiritual Universe" is just one example of several in which he dabbled in and explored scientific theories and themes at least a century before it was commonplace to do so. "Eureka" is one of many reasons some consider Poe a "time traveler."

Poe loved whiskey and absinthe, which are the two star ingredients in the classic Sazerac cocktail. The Sazerac was created in New Orleans around the time that Poe was writing most of his stories. This Sazerac, dedicated to Poe, gets a twist of lemon-thyme ice.

Fill a skull ice-cube mold or a large block ice-cube mold with water and the lemon thyme. Freeze until solid.

Once the ice is ready, place the whiskey and absinthe in a chilled rocks glass with the lemon-thyme ice. Using a cocktail stirrer, stir to combine. Garnish with the pansy and lemon peel.

SPLENDOROUS SIPS AND ILLIMITABLE MIXES

I repeat, therefore, that it must have been simply a freak of my own fancy, distempered by good Captain Hardy's green tea. Just before dawn, on each of the two nights of which I speak, I distinctly heard Mr. Wyatt replace the lid upon the oblong box, and force the nails into their old places by means of the muffled mallet. Having done this, he issued from his state-room, fully dressed, and proceeded to call Mrs. W. from hers.

—"THE OBLONG BOX"

The Oblong Box COCKTAIL

8 ounces lemon-lime soda
4 ounces green tea, chilled
2 ounces gin
½ ounce fresh lemon juice
2 sprigs fresh mint
2 lemon peels

MAKES 2 SERVINGS

This cocktail is made with green tea, which Poe describes the effects of in his 1844 short story "The Oblong Box."

Combine the soda, tea, gin, and lemon juice in a cocktail shaker filled with ice. Shake for 30 revolutions. Strain into a chilled coupe glass and garnish with the mint and lemon peel.

SPLENDOROUS SIPS AND ILLIMITABLE MIXES

> *U*pon the quiet mountain top,
> Steals drowsily and musically
> Into the universal valley.
> The rosemary nods upon the grave;
> —"THE SLEEPER"

The Sleeper:
RASPBERRY-ROSEMARY SHRUB MARGARITA

½ teaspoon pink Himalayan sea salt
Juice of 1 lime
6 ounces lemon-lime soda
2 ounces tequila
1 ounce Raspberry-Rosemary Shrub (page 131)
1 ounce orange liqueur
2 fresh raspberries
1 large sprig fresh rosemary

MAKES 1 SERVING

Poe shined a spotlight on rosemary in his 1831 poem, "The Sleeper." Rosemary stars in this shrub recipe. It is a perfect flavor combination with raspberries, accenting the fruit with a bit of delicious pungency.

A shrub cocktail ingredient is a mix of equal parts fresh fruit, honey or sugar, and vinegar. Shrubs ferment when they are set aside for approximately two weeks. It is the vinegar in the mixture that helps off-season fruits continue to provide their robust flavors in cocktails and punches. Shrubs were commonplace in and around Poe's Philadelphia. Today, and in recent years, the antiquated syrups have been enjoying a modern-day surge of popularity in everything from mojitos to margaritas. This recipe is for a margarita with a punch of pungent flavor from a raspberry-rosemary shrub.

Place the salt on a plate. Run the cut lime around the rim of the glass. Roll the rim of the glass in the salt. Place the lime juice, soda, tequila, shrub, and orange liqueur in a cocktail shaker filled with ice and shake for 30 revolutions. Strain into the prepared glass. Spear the raspberries onto the rosemary sprig and garnish the drink with it.

SPLENDOROUS SIPS AND ILLIMITABLE MIXES

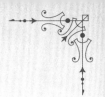

RASPBERRY-ROSEMARY SHRUB

2 cups fresh raspberries
¼ cup chopped fresh rosemary
3 cups apple cider vinegar
¼ cup honey

MAKES 20 SERVINGS

Shrubs—mixtures of vinegar, sugar, and fruit—were very popular in the 1840s. There are many ways to use shrubs in recipes, including cocktail recipes.

Place the raspberries in a large jar with a lid and use a fork to mash them. Add the rosemary and vinegar. Seal the jar and let sit in a cool, dark place for at least 2 weeks.

Strain the contents of the jar into a bowl through a fine-mesh sieve or cheesecloth. Use a wire whisk to combine the honey with the raspberry vinegar.

A freshly made shrub will last in an airtight container in the refrigerator for up to 6 months.

I couldn't make out her name at first; for, when she gave it in answer to my inquiry, it sounded like Beltot, which didn't sound right. But, when we became better acquainted—which was while Charker and I were drinking sugar-cane sangaree, which she made in a most excellent manner—I found that her Christian name was Isabella . . .
—"THE PERILS OF CERTAIN ENGLISH PRISONERS," BY CHARLES DICKENS

SANGAREE

2 ounces gin
1 ounce port
Pinch of freshly grated nutmeg

MAKES 1 SERVING

Poe is said to have loved port wine. A classic sangaree is a combination of port and gin. It was a highly fashionable mixed drink around the time Dickens visited Philadelphia. Dickens featured the sangaree in his 1857 novel *The Perils of Certain English Prisoners*.

Combine the gin and port in a cocktail shaker filled with ice. Shake for 30 revolutions and strain into a fluted glass. Garnish with a sprinkle of nutmeg.

> **HIDEOUS HINT**
>
> *Float a tiny herb or edible flower blossom in the drink.*

*Ever with thee I wish to roam—
Dearest my life is thine.
Give me a cottage for my home
And a rich old cypress vine,
Removed from the world with its sin and care
And the tattling of many tongues.
Love alone shall guide us when we are there—
Love shall heal my weakened lungs;
And oh, the tranquil hours we'll spend,
Never wishing that others may see!
Perfect ease we'll enjoy, without thinking to lend
Ourselves to the world and its glee—
Ever peaceful and blissful we'll be.*

—VIRGINIA CLEMM, FEBRUARY 14, 1846

Sissy's SYLLABUB

20 ounces apple cider
4 ounces milk
1 teaspoon vanilla extract
¼ cup sugar
6 cups ice
8 ounces heavy whipping cream, whipped until stiff peaks are formed
1 tablespoon ground cinnamon
1 teaspoon ground nutmeg (optional)
1 teaspoon ground cardamom
3 star anise
16 cinnamon sticks

MAKES 16 SERVINGS

Poe's wife, Virginia Clemm, wrote this poem for him for Valentine's Day in 1846. Her poem is an acrostic: the first letters of each line strung together spell out Edgar Allan Poe. This recipe for Victorian-era syllabub is dedicated to Virginia, whom Poe lovingly called Sissy. She passed away at the age of just twenty-four after a long battle with tuberculosis.

Combine the apple cider, milk, and vanilla, and stir until well blended. Use a large spoon to drop spoonfuls of the heavy whipping cream on top of the cider mixture, and gently fold the cream into the mixture. Add the ice.

In a small bowl, use a small spoon to combine the ground spices. Sprinkle the ground spices on top of the cider. The spices will rest on the cream, providing color contrast and light, wintery flavors.

Add the star anise on top. Place a cinnamon stick in each glass for guests to use as a flavorful stirrer.

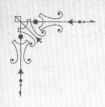

> *A*stounding news! ... The Atlantic crossed in three days! Signal triumph of Mr. Monck Mason's flying machine!!!
>
> —"THE BALLOON HOAX"

Mr. Monck Mason's Flying Machine
CHAMPAGNE COCKTAIL

6 ounces Champagne, chilled

1½ ounces apple brandy

¼ teaspoon freshly grated nutmeg

Thin apple slice, to perch on the rim

1 cinnamon stick

MAKES 1 SERVING

Poe's 1844 hoax story in *The New York Sun* falsely announced—and convinced New Yorkers—that a hot-air balloon was making a three-day Atlantic crossing.

This cocktail is made with Champagne, which is a customary drink following a hot-air balloon ride. These apple-cinnamon flavors would be perfect for a leaf-peeping hot-air balloon ride.

Pour the Champagne into a chilled Champagne flute. Add the apple brandy and use a cocktail stirrer to combine. Garnish with a sprinkle of nutmeg, thin apple slice, and serve a cinnamon stick on the side.

SPLENDOROUS SIPS AND ILLIMITABLE MIXES

I became possessed with the keenest curiosity about the whirl itself . . . and my principal grief was that I should never be able to tell my old companions on shore about the mysteries I should see.

—"A DESCENT INTO THE MAELSTROM"

Descent into the Maelstrom Punch: PHILADELPHIA FISH-HOUSE PUNCH

Ice
48 ounces red-berry fruit punch

Punch
12 ounces Armagnac brandy
8 ounces dark rum
8 ounces peach liqueur
8 ounces cognac
2 large fresh lemons
3 fresh limes
8 maraschino cherries, stems on

Specialty Tools
10-inch carp-shaped cake pan
8 bamboo cocktail skewers

MAKES 24 SERVINGS

Poe's 1841 short story "A Descent into the Maelstrom" is about a man who survives a shipwreck. The ice in this punch resembles the fish he encountered. The ice chills the punch, which is a medley of rum, brandy, and citrus inspired by the antebellum classic Philadelphia Fish-House Punch. Records dating as far back as 1732 show that members of the Schuylkill Fishing Club in Philadelphia sipped on Philadelphia Fish-House Punch at their meetings.

To make the ice: At least 1 day before you plan to serve the punch, place the cake pan in the freezer and place bunched-up pieces of aluminum foil where needed to steady the mold. When the mold is steady, use a cup to fill it with the fruit juice while it is in the freezer. The juice will melt into the punch to create a delicious flavor and texture.

To make the punch: Combine the brandy, rum, peach liqueur, and cognac in a large punch bowl and stir. Squeeze the juice from 1 of the lemons and 1 of the limes into the mixture. Slice the remaining lemon and limes into thin slices; discard the ends. Add the ice to the punch bowl. Use the cocktail skewers to secure the cherries to the lemon slices, stems up. Float these and the lime slices in the punch.

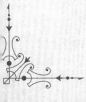

SPLENDOROUS SIPS AND ILLIMITABLE MIXES

No thinking being lives who, at some luminous point of his life of thought, has not felt himself lost amid the surges of futile efforts at understanding, or believing, that anything exists greater than his own soul.

—"EUREKA"

Eureka PUNCH

Poe's 1848 prose poem "Eureka" grappled with his wonderment over the universe. It was his last published nonfiction work. A crescent moon and star made by freezing juices in cake molds decorate and add flavor and color to this party punch. This recipe is based on the golden rule of ratio for party punches: one of sour, two of sweet, three of strong, four of weak.

Ice
5 cups grape juice
5 cups mango-pineapple juice

Punch
16 ounces orange liqueur
32 ounces lemonade
48 ounces Champagne
56 ounces lemon-lime soda
7 small leaves fresh or dried scented geranium

Specialty Tools
Crescent moon–shaped silicone cake pan, 8½ x 3 x 2 inches
8-inch five-pointed star-shaped aluminum cake pan

MAKES 24 SERVINGS

To make the ice: At least 1 day before serving the punch, place the cake pans in the freezer and place bunched-up pieces of aluminum foil where needed to steady the mold. When the molds are steady, use a cup to fill the moon mold with grape juice. Fill the star mold with the mango-pineapple juice. The juices will melt into the punch to create delicious flavor and texture.

To make the punch: Place the liqueur, lemonade, Champagne, and soda in a large punch bowl and stir to combine. Add the ice. Garnish with the geranium leaves.

  SPLENDOROUS SIPS AND ILLIMITABLE MIXES

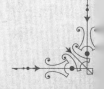

*H*ot punch is a pleasant thing, gentlemen—an extremely pleasant thing under any circumstances—but in that snug old parlor, before the roaring fire, with the wind blowing outside till every timber in the old house creaked again, Tom Smart found it perfectly delightful.

—CHARLES DICKENS

APPLE HOT PUNCH

1 ounce rum
1 ounce cognac
¼ teaspoon fresh lemon juice
1 cup boiling water
1 cinnamon stick
1 Mini Chocolate Skull (page 111)

MAKES 1 SERVING

At one time, Poe called Charles Dickens "the greatest British novelist." The two writers met twice in 1842 while Dickens visited Philadelphia. One visit was on March 6, presumably where Dickens was staying at the United States Hotel, which was on Chestnut Street, between 4th and 5th Streets. What did they drink? Very possibly, they sipped on the hot punch drinks that Dickens mentioned numerous times in his writings. Dickens's hot punch is a soothing blend of fresh lemon, rum, and cognac mixed with boiling water. It would have been the perfect tipple on a chilly winter day. Serve this apple rum variation in a pretty clear-glass punch cup with a mini chocolate skull stuck on a cinnamon stick for a stirrer.

Combine the rum, cognac, and lemon juice in a punch cup or mug. Add 1 cup of boiling water and stir. Add the cinnamon stick, topped with a mini chocolate skull, to use as a stirrer.

SPLENDOROUS SIPS AND ILLIMITABLE MIXES 141

Get a couple of sherry-cobblers, Mark, and we'll drink success to the firm. "This wonderful invention, sir," said Mark, tenderly patting the empty glass, "is called a cobbler. Sherry cobbler when you name it long; cobbler, when you name it short. Now you're equal to having your boots took off, and are, in every particular worth mentioning, another man."
—THE LIFE AND ADVENTURES OF MARTIN CHUZZLEWIT, BY CHARLES DICKENS

BLUEBERRY SHERRY COBBLER

1 cup crushed ice
3 ounces sherry
6 large blueberries, muddled, plus 2 large blueberries for garnish
1 tablespoon maple syrup
1 orange wheel, halved
1 sprig mint on a strong stem

MAKES 1 SERVING

Mix sherry, citrus, and sugar together in a glass filled with crushed ice, and you have a Sherry Cobbler. It's one of the world's first-ever "highball" cocktails. The year after he first experienced this trendy drink on a visit to Philadelphia (the same visit when he met with Poe) Charles Dickens spotlighted the Sherry Cobbler in his 1844 novel *The Life and Adventures of Martin Chuzzlewit*.

Combine the ice, sherry, muddled blueberries, maple syrup, and half of the orange wheel in a cocktail shaker and shake for 30 revolutions. Strain into a highball glass filled with the remaining crushed ice. Garnish with the remaining half orange wheel and 2 blueberries on a mint sprig.

HIDEOUS HINT

Place red cake-decorating gel "blood drips" around the rim of the glass. Place a lychee stuffed with a blueberry on a bamboo cocktail skewer on the side of the glass to form an eyeball. (See Icy Air of Night Fruit Platter on page 31.)

142　SPLENDOROUS SIPS AND ILLIMITABLE MIXES

One or two strokes of a spade upturned the blade of a large Spanish knife, and, as we dug farther, three or four loose pieces of gold and silver coin came to light.

—"THE GOLD-BUG"

William Legrand's Gold-Bug COCKTAIL

3 ounces cinnamon schnapps
1 tablespoon edible gold luster dust
3 ounces Champagne
2 ounces orange Cognac

MAKES 2 SERVINGS

HIDEOUS HINT

Float a tiny edible flower blossom in the drink.

Poe's 1843 short story "The Gold-Bug" is about an invisible message written on a gold-bug, revealing where Captain Kidd buried his treasure some two hundred years earlier. Edible gold luster dust makes this sparkly schnapps and Champagne cocktail glimmer.

Use some of the schnapps to wet the rim of the glass. Place the edible gold luster dust on a plate and spread it thinly across the plate. Place the rim of the glass on the luster dust and roll it twice to cover the rim with the dust.

Combine the schnapps, Champagne, and Cognac in a cocktail shaker filled with ice and shake for 30 revolutions. Strain into a Champagne glass and sprinkle edible gold luster dust on top.

SPLENDOROUS SIPS AND ILLIMITABLE MIXES

My general proposition, then, is this:—In the original unity of the first thing lies the secondary cause of all things, with the germ of their Inevitable annihilation.

—"EUREKA"

The Big-Bang LAVENDER WATER

¼ cup fresh or dried lavender buds
3 large limes
36 ounces lemon-lime soda
12 sprigs fresh or dried lavender

Specialty Tools
Ice cube tray
4 tincture bottles
4 laboratory beakers
4 Tom Collins glasses

MAKES 4 SERVINGS

As he tinkered with the theory of evolution, Poe was an advocate of many great Victorian scientists. He dedicated his poem "Eureka," in which he examines how the universe was established, to Victorian naturalist Alexander von Humboldt.

To make this lavender water, guests will use tincture bottles to add lavender to soda water, as if they were conducting a science experiment. Lavender flowers frozen in small ice cubes are released into the water as the ice melts, adding more flavor. Order dried culinary lavender online or grow lavender and dry it.

Fill an ice cube tray with water and sprinkle half of the lavender buds over the water. Freeze at least overnight, longer if needed.

Distribute the juice from 2 or 3 of the limes equally among the tincture bottles. Place the remaining half of the lavender buds in the laboratory beakers, spreading them equally among the beakers. Place the soda and lavender ice cubes in each Tom Collins glass. Cut 4 thin round slices from the remaining lime, and then cut a ½ inch into each round and place on the rim of each glass as a garnish. Tuck 3 lavender sprigs under each lime wheel. Provide a tincture, a beaker, and a glass to each guest for them to assemble their cocktail. Encourage guests to enjoy experimenting with different amounts of lime, soda, and lavender.

SPLENDOROUS SIPS AND ILLIMITABLE MIXES

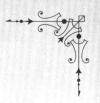

But the freedom that they fought for, and the country grand they wrought for, is their monument today, and for aye.

—THOMAS DUNN ENGLISH

MILK PUNCH

1 cup ice
8 ounces whole milk
1½ ounces apple brandy
¼ teaspoon freshly grated nutmeg

MAKES 1 SERVING

Milk spiked with brandy or whiskey, a cocktail known as milk punch, became popular in the 1700s. In the mid-1800s, contemporary spins on the classic milk punch recipe took root. One variation that caught on feverishly was by New Jersey politician Thomas Dunn English, who was a friend of Poe's. Here is a simple recipe for a delicious, cold and creamy milk punch with freshly grated nutmeg.

Place the ice, milk, and brandy in a rocks glass. Add the nutmeg and stir to combine.

SPLENDOROUS SIPS AND ILLIMITABLE MIXES

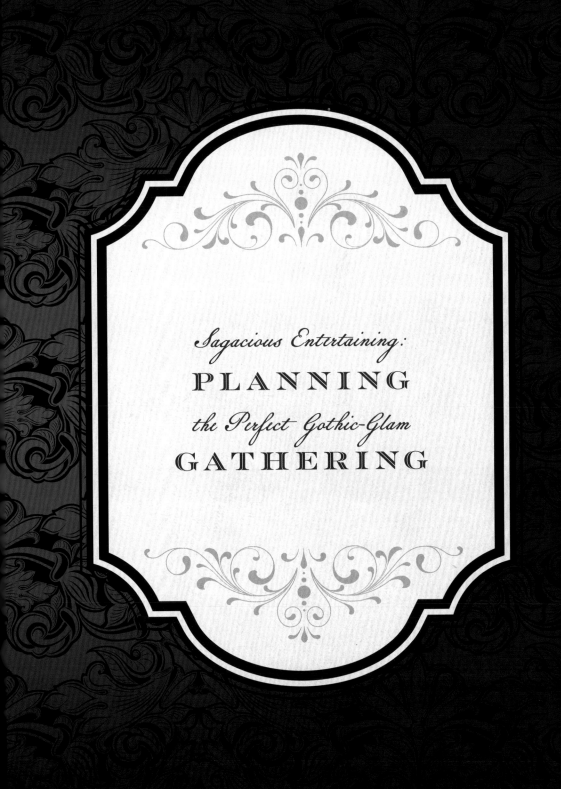

Sagacious Entertaining:
PLANNING
the Perfect Gothic-Glam
GATHERING

GOTHIC FETES AND FESTIVALS

These party planning ideas are intended to help make the most of your gothic gathering. Everyone will appreciate the extra steps taken to ensure a memorable experience. These are inexpensive ways to capture the gothic atmosphere of the mid-nineteenth century.

- Dress in period clothing or in a costume inspired by a Poe story. Encourage guests to also consider theme dress and period outfits by including a message in the invitation.

- Decorate with plenty of silk flowers in black, deep purple, and other morose colors.

- Transform the atmosphere with eye-catching visuals. Make stencils to decorate the tops of cakes, cookies, and more by covering the top of a cookie cutter with parchment paper and securing it all around with tape. Sprinkle powdered sugar, cocoa powder, cake decorating sprinkles and more over the covered cookie cutter, creating the outline of a shape. Be sure to get the powder or sprinkles up close against the edge of the cookie cutter. Eye-catching visuals will transform the atmosphere.

- Consider hosting at least some of the gathering by candlelight.

- Make the party an interpretive learning event by placing the name of someone from the mid-1800s on the back of each guest. Ask them to try to guess who they are by asking other guests "yes" or "no" questions about the person.

- Play Edgar Allan Poe movies on TV screens throughout the house, with the sound off, to reinforce the gothic imagery.

- Encourage guests to study up on the many words and phrases Poe invented or used and challenge them to see how many words they can use throughout the gathering.

- Use vials and laboratory beakers to present condiments and garnishes.

- Fresh herbs bring dishes and displays together. Arrange rosemary, sage, and thyme in centerpieces, elaborate cakes, and candle arrangements. Make dining interactive by allowing guests to pick out and cut their own herbs for garnishes.

- Chill punch with ice molded in skull- and raven-shaped silicone cake pans.

- Entertain with gothic-themed trivia, cryptography code challenges, and card games and songs that were popular in the 1840s. (See following pages for details.)

- Colored cake-decorating gels and sprays can be used to simulate blood drips and splotches on foods.

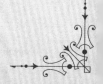

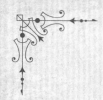

- Present foods in little wooden coffins and skulls.

- Make a centerpiece Edgar Allan Poe story-themed cake like the Cask of Amontillado Dessert Wall featured on page 100.

- Capture the environment of the period with framed silhouettes, which were popular in the 1840s before photographs were widely available.

- Encourage guests to dress up with a costume contest. Create a period photo booth and take photos of guests to enclose in the thank-you note you send after the gathering.

Hideous Hints and Ideas

- Eyeballs are a recurring theme in Poe's stories. Make eyeball garnishes and accents for dishes and throughout centerpieces and other party décor. Use bamboo cocktail sticks to secure blueberries to lychees or olives inside cherry peppers and cheese balls.

- Use a paring knife to carve ominous eyes and mouths into potatoes, bell peppers, roasted squash, melons, and puff pastry dough. For more dimension, place olives and mozzarella balls in eye sockets.

- Garnish cocktails with bite-size pieces of fruits like furry kiwi and spike-covered kiwano melons.

- Make bite-size spooky cutout cookies (page 110) to serve with drinks. Bake the cookies first and carve eyes and mouths with a paring knife or use cookie cutters and silicone molds to form shapes.

- Use miniature cookie cutters to create tiny spooky cutouts in pie crusts to place on cakes and pies.

- Select dark-colored flowers for the table and in rooms where guests will be entertained.

- Shop for themed dishes. You don't need a whole set, just a few accent pieces.

- Use stencils and cardamom, cocoa powder, or powdered sugar to add spooky images to cakes and breads.

- Black, deep purple, or silver cake-decorating spray can be applied to a variety of surfaces, not just cakes.

- Red cake-decorating gel can be used to draw bloodshot eyes, inflamed veins, and blood drips.

- Create blood spatter with red food coloring or red berry jellies or jams.

- Inexpensive skull-shaped jars can be used to serve food, present condiments, or so guests can take home leftover party foods and treats.

DOS AND DON'TS OF VICTORIAN ENTERTAINING

Do	Don't
Eat your food slowly.	Never fill your mouth and never open your mouth while chewing.
After dinner, ladies should retreat to the drawing room for coffee or tea, allowing the men to smoke.	Never leave food lingering on your whiskers. Use a napkin to wipe away food discreetly.
Arrive on time. Some believe it is best not to show up at all rather than be late. Arriving early, which could distract a host, should also be avoided.	Don't focus on the food. Find other topics for discussion.
A good hostess should be tactful in planning the seating arrangement. Seat a "good talker" in the center of the table. Distance people who are known to have differences.	Never encourage people to take more food than they seem willing to eat.
Remove gloves at the table.	Never dip bread into gravy on your plate.
Gentlemen should stand behind their chairs until ladies are seated.	Never apologize for food served. This could be perceived as coaxing a compliment.
Keep conversation light and positive. Avoid controversial topics.	Never smell or examine the food.

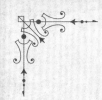

TRIALED TRIVIA QUESTIONS

1. IN WHICH CITY WAS POE LAST SEEN ALIVE?

   a. Philadelphia
   b. Boston
   c. Richmond
   d. Baltimore

2. WHICH OF THESE IS POE'S MOST FAMOUS WORK?

   a. "The Cask of Amontillado"
   b. "The Tell-Tale Heart"
   c. "The Raven"
   d. "The Masque of the Red Death"

3. WHAT WAS THE NAME OF POE'S WIFE?

   a. Maria
   b. Virginia
   c. Lenore
   d. Berenice

4. TRUE OR FALSE?
   POE WAS ORPHANED AND ADOPTED.

5. WHICH OF THESE WAS POE'S FIRST PUBLISHED WORK?

   a. *Tamerlane and Other Poems*
   b. "The Fall of the House of Usher"
   c. "Berenice"
   d. "Ligeia"

6. WHAT IS THE NAME OF THE CITY WHERE POE WAS BORN?

   a. Boston
   b. Philadelphia
   c. Richmond
   d. New York

7. WHICH OF THESE UNIVERSITIES DID POE ATTEND?

   a. Harvard
   b. University of Virginia
   c. Princeton
   d. Penn State

ANSWERS
1) d; 2) c; 3) b; 4) True; 5) a; 6) a; 7) b

SAGACIOUS ENTERTAINING

CRYPTOGRAPHY GAME

Poe loved cryptography, the challenge of decoding message "ciphers" by guessing letters. He called it "secret writing." In his 1843 short story "The Gold-Bug," the gold-bug has a cipher that reveals the location of buried treasure.

As a newspaper editor, Poe invited readers to submit ciphers for other readers to solve. Purportedly, there was only one cipher from a reader that Poe could not solve, which was finally solved in 2020.

There are smartphone applications that help create ciphers. Have fun with your guests by asking them to create ciphers in advance for other guests to decode at your Victorian party.

The Raven

A	B	C	D	E	F	G	H	I	J	K	L	M	N	O	P	Q	R	S	T	U	V	W	X	Y	Z
B	P	F	Y	X	U	V	Z	N	D	T	R	I	A	M	G	O	W	E	H	J	S	C	K	Q	L

Challenge

Y	B	W	T	A	X	E	E

H	Z	X	W	X

B	A	Y

A	M	H	Z	N	A	V

I	M	W	X

Answers

N	O	T	H	I	N	G
A	M	H	Z	N	A	V

M	O	R	E
I	M	W	X

D	A	R	K	N	E	S	S
Y	B	W	T	A	X	E	E

T	H	E	R	E
H	Z	X	W	X

A	N	D
B	A	Y

HOW TO HOST A MEDIEVAL MURDER-MYSTERY DINNER PARTY

Poe's 1842 short story "The Masque of the Red Death" takes place in a medieval abbey. A few simple steps can transform your home into the perfect place to have a party.

1. Set a theme. Come up with a theme for your party and share the theme with invited guests well ahead of the gathering. This will provide time for them to prepare and then enjoy the party more. Make your theme a costume contest or a competition to see which of your friends makes the best home-brewed craft mead, an alcoholic drink that was popular in medieval times. It is made by fermenting fruits, spices, grains, or hops in honey and water.

2. Send invitations. Send invitations as early as possible to give guests time to plan. Send an eye-catching card in the mail with an engaging message underscoring the theme of the party. If time allows, hand-deliver invitations, dressed in medieval clothing. Include a QR code that leads to an electronic invitation so guests can plug the address, time, and other details into their smartphones.

3. Plan a medieval menu. In this entertaining guide, there are delicious recipes for hearty turkey drumsticks, mulled wine, and other popular medieval foods. Plan to have plenty of basic fruits (grapes, apples) and vegetables (carrots, beans), nuts, olives, cheeses, and biscuits as well. Make cutout cookies (page 110) in the shape of swords, flags, and shields.

4. Create a centerpiece. Create an eye-catching centerpiece that somehow tells the story of the Middle Ages. Whether it's flowers, fresh fruit, an arrangement of candles, or a combination of all three, spend time and creative muscle on the centerpiece. It will bring everything together, reinforcing the theme. Order a plastic shield, flag, or sword online and build an arrangement around it of flowers, candles, and tapestries. There can't be too many candelabras. An elaborate cake, like the Prince Prospero's Uninvited Guest Cake (page 92), can be a conversation-starting centerpiece. Try to use the colors yellow, red, and blue as much as possible.

5. Have a photo booth. Construct an inexpensive backdrop where guests can pose for photos. This can be made with anything from plants to fabric to construction paper. Take photos of guests and send the photos to them later with a thank-you note.

SAGACIOUS ENTERTAINING 157

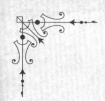

HOW TO PLAY POE'S FAVORITE CARD GAMES

Three-Card Loo

One of the most popular card games in the 1840s was three-card Loo. Loo is a shortened version of the name Lanterlu, which is how the game was known when it was developed in England in the 1700s. Loo remained fashionable in the United States in the nineteenth century, but lost relevance in the twentieth century. Loo is a gambling game that can be played with five to nine players. Each player receives three cards. After seeing their cards, each player must either play their hand or fold them. If they play their hand, the goal is to win at least one trick. If they don't win a trick they are "looed," meaning they must add to a central pool of chips. Players that win tricks accumulate chips from the pool. The winner is the player with the most tricks.

7 Up

The card game 7Up was also popular in the 1800s. 7Up is played with a fifty-two-card deck and at least two players. Each player receives seven cards initially. Remaining cards are set face down in the center of the game table. Players pull cards from the cards in the center. The goal of each player is to get rid of their cards. The player to the left of the dealer shows a card. If the next player cannot show a card that is one rank higher or one rank lower, they have to pull a card from the deck in the middle. The first player to get rid of all their cards wins.

SONG LIST

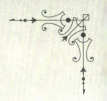

Music is so essential to a gathering, and we can connect with people better when we hear the songs from their lifetime. Here is a playlist of songs to share that were the most popular when Poe was most active in his work. The first list, the most recent, is from 1849, which is when Poe passed away due to unknown circumstances.

1849

"Dolcy Jones"

"Nelly Was a Lady"

"Once in Royal David's City"

"Santa Lucia"

1846

"There's a Good Time Coming"

"Well-A-Day"

"When the Swallows Homeward Fly"

1843

"Columbia, the Gem of the Ocean"

"I Dreamt I Dwelt in Marble Halls"
(from the opera *The Bohemian Girl*)

"Old Dan Tucker"

1840

"The Old Arm Chair"

"Lay a Garland"

1837

"Hark, Brothers, Hark"

"Woodman, Spare That Tree!"

ACKNOWLEDGMENTS

I would like to extend sincere thanks to Chris Semtner, curator of the Edgar Allan Poe Museum in Richmond, Virginia, for the wonderful conversation and information. Thank you for your passion and dedication in getting these stories told. Thanks to Bruce Conard and the team at Festival Foods in Wausau, Wisconsin, where so many hard-to-find spirits and wines are available because of your expertise and caring. Thanks to Melissa Lauer with Fraunces Tavern Museum. Thank you to US Park Service Historian Stefan Kosovych and Curator Karie Diethorn, both with Edgar Allan Poe National Historic Site in Philadelphia, for providing reference materials and distinctly knowledgeable sources for this book. Thank you to the Edgar Allan Poe Society of Baltimore for maintaining Poe's resting place and making it accessible to all. To visit is to understand the significance of this literary hero. Special thanks to the many people who have been instrumental in this book project: Kelly Alexis, Edward Ash-Milby, Kayla Belser, Kristi Visser, Katie Killebrew, Debra-Ann Brabazon, Joanna Broder, Sara Burrows, Janna Childs, Mary Corrado, Barbara Culhane, Alicia Dale, Sheryl DeVore, Katherine Ferrera, Mary Graham, Janice Harper, Bill Hinke, Dave Hinke, Elaine Hinke, Jeanne Hinke, Jeff Hinke, Kayla Kohlmeister, Robert Kowalski, Woody Leake, Paul McPolin, Ann Michlig, Catherine Mio Anderson, Tim Moriarty, Joyce Nick, Alex Novak, Nityia Przewlocki, Ruth L. Ratny, Jenny Thomas, Cathy Tréboux, Greg Venne, Joel Weber, Marilee Wright, and Denis Stencil.

BIBLIOGRAPHY

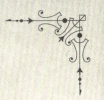

BOOKS & ARTICLES

Barué, Sulpice. *Domestic French Cookery*, 4th edition. 2011.

Collins, Paul. *Edgar Allan Poe: The Fever Called Living*. Houghton, Mifflin, Harcourt. 2014.

Cullen, Lynn. *Mrs. Poe*. Gallery Books. 2014.

Dickens, Charles. *Adventures of Martin Chuzzlewit*. Oxford University Press; Reissue edition. 2009.

Edwards, Phil. "Afraid of Being Buried Alive? These Coffins Are for You." Vox. July 31, 2015.

Glasse, Hannah. *The Art of Cookery Made Plain and Easy*. Townsends, 9th edition. 2018.

Grossman, Jo. Weibezahl, Robert. *A Second Helping of Murder*. Poisoned Pen Press. 2003.

Hine, Mary Anne. Marshall, Gordon. Weaver, William Woys. *The Larder Invaded: Reflections on Three Centuries of Philadelphia Food and Drink*. The Library Company of Philadelphia. 1987.

Hutchisson, James M. *Poe*. University Press of Mississippi. 2005.

Kelly, Helena. *The Life and Lies of Charles Dickens*. Pegasus Books, Ltd. 2023.

Leslie, Eliza. *The Lady's Receipt-Book: A Useful Companion for Large or Small Families*. Carey and Hart. 1847.

Meyers, Jeffrey. *Edgar Allan Poe: His Life and Legacy*. First Cooper Square Press edition. 2000.

Nelson, Max. "The Machinery of the Universe." The Paris Review. July 1, 2015.

O'Brien, Sam. "The Death of Pennsylvania's Forgotten Funeral Pie." Atlas Obscura. August 22, 2022.

Poe, Edgar Allan. *Edgar Allan Poe Classic Stories*. Sterling Publishing Company, Inc. 2018.

Poe, Edgar Allan. *Edgar Allan Poe: The Ultimate Collection*. Enhanced Media Publishing. 2016.

Price, Vincent. *Cooking Price-Wise: A Culinary Legacy*. Calla Editions; Expanded edition. 2017.

Quinn, Arthur Hobson. *Edgar Allan Poe: A Critical Biography*. The Johns Hopkins University Press. 1998.

Randolph, Mary. *The Virginia Housewife*. 1993.

Segan, Francine. "Digging into the Sweet History of Sicilian Cannoli." La Cucina Italiana. November 10, 2020.

Seldon, Cele and Lynn. "Partake of the Palmetto State: What to Eat in South Carolina." FoodNetwork.com.

Semtner, Christopher. "Poe in Richmond: Poe's Tell-Tale Hair at the Poe Museum." Autumn 2017.

Staib, Walter. *The City Tavern Cookbook: Recipes from The Birthplace of American Cuisine*. Running Press. 2009.

Tarazano, D. Lawrence. "People Feared Being Buried Alive So Much They Invented These Special Safety Coffins." Smithsonian Magazine.

BLOGS

Gray, Elizabeth Kelly. "Was Edgar Allan Poe a Habitual Opium User?" Common Place Online.

Moskovitz, Herb. "Charles Dickens and Edgar Allan Poe in Philadelphia: A Literary Meeting." May 25, 2013.

Poe, Virginia Clemm. "Valentine to Edgar Allan Poe." February 14, 1846. EAPoe.org (Edgar Allan Poe Society of Baltimore).

"Vincent's Kitchen." VincentPriceLegacy.com.

"Vincent Price Cooks!" LadyCultBlog.com. January 14, 2019.

INDEX

3D skull ice-cube mold, 126
7Up card game, 158

A

Alarum Premature Burial Fruit-Pastry Bites, 38–39
alcohol beverages, 118–147
 The Big-Bang Lavender Water, 146
 Blueberry Sherry Cobbler, 142–143
 Descent into the Maelstrom Punch, 138–139
 Eureka Punch, 140
 Milk Punch, 147
 Mr. Monck Mason's Flying Machine Champagne Cocktail, 136–137
 The Oblong Box Cocktail, 128–129
 The Pit and the Pendulum Spanish Coffee, 126
 Poe Family Eggnog, 122–123
 Prince Prospero's Angel of the Odd Kirsch Mulled Wine with Chokeberries, 120–121
 Raspberry-Rosemary Shrub, 131
 Sangaree, 132–133
 Sissy's Syllabub, 134–135
 The Sleeper, 130
 The Time Traveler, 126
 Tintinnabulation Tea Blend, 124–125
 William Legrand's Gold-Bug Cocktail, 144–145
American antebellum period (1832–1860), 7, 11, 13
anchovy toast, 41
"Annabel Lee" poem, 62–63
Annabel Lee's Crab Bisque, 62–63
appetizers, 15–43
 Alarum Premature Burial Fruit-Pastry Bites, 38–39
 Arthur Gordon Pym's Black-Tree Candy Bark, 40
 Boundaries of Life and Death Party Dip, 16–17
 C. August Dupin's Charcuterie Board, 18–20
 Forest Reverie Butter Board, 24–25
 Fortunato's Stuffed Médoc Mushrooms, 35
 House of Usher Party Crackers, 22–23
 Icy Air of Night Fruit Platter, 30–31
 Patatas Bravas, 36–37
 Pit and the Pendulum Bread, 28–29
 The Poe Toaster's Anchovy Toast Points, 41
 Roasted Apricots and Bananas Raven Food, 42
 Sinbad the Sailor's Roasted Carrot and Blood-Orange Hummus Boats, 21
 Some Words with a Mummy Appetizer, 26–27
 Tavern Biscuits, 34
 Tea Cakes, 43
 Vulture-Eye Deviled Eggs, 32–33
apple brandy, 136–137, 147
apple cider vinegar
 Raspberry-Rosemary Shrub, 131
 Sissy's Syllabub, 134–135
 Vinegar Pie, 112
apples
 Apple Compote, 108–109, 110
 Apple Hot Punch, 141
 The Assignation Salad, 48
apricots, 42
Armagnac Brandied Peaches, 103
Armagnac brandy, 103, 138–139
Arthur Gordon Pym's Black-Tree Candy Bark, 40
Arthur Gordon Pym's Clam Chowder, 54–55
"The Assignation" short story, 48, 58–59

B

"The Balloon Hoax" newspaper article, 138
bananas, 42
Barbarous Islanders' Lobster Newberg, 70–71
bark, 40
beans, 82
Beef Wellington, 68–69
"The Bells" poem, 30–31, 124
"Berenice" short story, 86, 89
Berenice Teeth, 89
berries. See blackberries; cherries; chokeberries; cranberries; raspberries; strawberries
"The Big-Bang Lavender Water, 146
biscuits, 34
Black Beans Cakes, 82
black rice, 50–51, 83
black sesame seeds, 22–23
black tea, 124–125
blackberries, 18–20, 60–61
Black-Tree Candy Bark, 40
blood oranges, 21
bloodlike decoration
 drips, 142–143
 pores, 120
 spatter, 31, 66–67, 126
 veins, 76–77
blueberries, 30–31, 142–143
Blueberry Sherry Cobbler, 142–143
Boundaries of Life and Death Party Dip (ham salad), 16–17
brandy, 103, 136–137, 138–139, 147
bread, 28–29, 52–53
Brie cheese, 18–20
bun cake, 92–94
bundt cake pan, 92–94
butter
 board, 24–25
 lemon compound, 76–77

butter nut squash, 46–47
buttercream frosting
 chocolate buttercream frosting, 88, 90–91, 94, 100–102
 vanilla buttercream frosting, 89, 99
butterfly pea-flower tea, 124–125

C

C. August Dupin's Charcuterie Board, 18–20
Cadaver Rice, 46–47
cake
 The Cask of Amontillado Dessert Wall, 100–102
 Graveyard Poke Cake, 86–88
 Ligeia Dream Cake, 106–107
 Prince Prospero's Uninvited Guest Cake, 92–94
 Shadow Cake, 104–105
 William Legrand's Gold-Bug Cake, 98–99
cake pans
 carp-shaped cake pan, 138–139
 castle-shaped bundt cake pan, 92–94
 crescent moon-shaped silicone cake pan, 140
 dome-shaped cake pan, 99
 skull cake pan, 30–31
 star-shaped aluminum cake pan, 140
candy bark, 40
cannoli, 116–117
card games, 158
carp-shaped cake pan, 138–139
carrots, 21
Cask of Amontillado Cannoli, 116–117
The Cask of Amontillado Dessert Wall, 100–102
"The Cask of Amontillado" short story, 35, 50, 60–61, 72, 100–102, 116–117, 122–123

castle-shaped bundt cake pan, 92–94
Catacombs Roasted Cauliflower, 72–73
Catacombs Roasted Zucchini and Black Rice with Bell Peppers, 50–51
cauliflower, 72–73
Champagne, 136–137, 140, 144–145
charcuterie board, 18–20
cheese
   Brie, 18–20
   cream cheese, 18–20, 30–31, 38–39, 48, 80
   Gouda, 26–27, 78–79
   mozzarella, 48, 57
   string cheese, 18–20
cherries, 42
Cherry-Cranberry Compote, 66–67, 74–75, 78
chicken, 83
chickpeas, 21
Chilled Blackberry Médoc Soup with Fresh Mint, 60–61
chocolate
   Chocolate Skulls, 111
   Chocolate Wall, 102
   feather-shaped silicone mold for, 76–77
   milk-chocolate bark, 40
   Mini Chocolate Skulls, 88, 108–109, 141
chocolate buttercream frosting, 88, 90–91, 94, 100–102
chokeberries, 120–121
chowder, 54–55
Cilantro Cream Cheese Tea Sandwiches, 80
Cilantro Crema, 82
cinnamon schnapps, 144–145
"The City in the Sea" poem, 94
The City in the Sea Violet Ice Cream, 95
clam chowder, 54–55
Clemm, Virginia, 135
coconut cake, 98–99

cod, 81
coffee, 126
coffins
   Graveyard Poke Cake, 86–87
   shaped cookie cutters, 38–39, 110
Cognac, 141, 144–145
compote
   Apple Compote, 108–109, 110
   cherry-cranberry compote, 66–67, 74–75
confetti, 40
cookie cutters
   coffin-shaped, 38–39, 110
   masquerade mask, 69
   quill-shaped, 60–61
   raven-shaped, 22–23, 104–105
   tombstone-shaped, 110
cookies
   Berenice Teeth (cookies and marshmallow dessert), 89
   Tombstone Cookies, 108–109, 110
crab bisque, 62–63
crackers, 22–23, 56
cranberries, 66–67, 74–75, 78
cream cheese
   Alarum Premature Burial Fruit-Pastry Bites, 38–39
   The Assignation Salad, 48
   C. August Dupin's Charcuterie Board, 18–20
   Ghost Pepper Jelly and Cilantro Cream Cheese Tea Sandwiches, 80
   Icy Air of Night Fruit Platter, 30–31
crescent moon-shaped silicone cake pan, 140
"The Cry of the Penny Pie Man" (Charles Dickens), 112
cryptography game, 155

D

Descent into the Maelstrom Hashed Cod, 81
Descent into the Maelstrom Punch, 138–139
"A Descent into the Maelstrom" short story, 81, 139
desserts, 84–117
   Apple Compote, 110
   Armagnac Brandied Peaches, 103
   Berenice Teeth, 89
   The Cask of Amontillado Dessert Wall, 100–102
   The City in the Sea Violet Ice Cream, 95
   Funeral Pie, 113
   Graveyard Poke Cake, 86–88
   The Hideous Heart Dessert, 90–91
   Lafourcade Family Graveyard Trifle, 108–109
   Lemon Pie, 112
   Ligeia Dream Cake, 106–107
   No-Churn ice cream, 96–97
   Paradise Pears, 114–115
   The Penny Pie Man's Pies, 112
   Prince Prospero's Uninvited Guest Cake, 92–94
   Shadow Cake, 104–105
   Tombstone Cookies, 110
   Vanilla Pudding, 111
   Vinegar Pie, 112
   William Legrand's Gold-Bug Cake, 98–99
deviled eggs, 32–33
Dickens, Charles, 132, 142
diet, of Poe, 10
dinner parties, 148–159
dips, 30–31
dome-shaped cake pan, 99
dragon fruit, 30–31
dressings, 48
dry red wine, 70–71
Dupin, C. Auguste, 8, 18–20

E

eggnog, 122–123
eggs, deviled, 32–33
"Eleanora" short story, 49
English, Thomas Dunn, 147
"Eureka" poem, 140, 146
Eureka Punch, 140
eyeball cake-decorating confetti, 40

F

"The Fall of the House of Usher" short story, 22–23, 46–47
feather-shaped silicone chocolate mold, 76–77
fennel, 48
fennel seeds, 22–23
festivals, 150–152
fillings, 38–39, 116–117
fish, cod, 81
floorboards, 90–91
Forest Reverie Butter Board, 24–25
"Forest Reverie" poem, 24–25
Fortunato's Stuffed Médoc Mushrooms, 35
frosting, 106–107
   chocolate buttercream frosting, 88, 90–91, 94, 100–102
   vanilla buttercream frosting, 89, 99
fruit dip, 30–31
fruit platter, 30–31
fruit-pastry bites, 38–39
Funeral Pie, 113

G

Gelatin Heart, 90–91
Ghost Pepper Jelly and Cilantro Cream Cheese Tea Sandwiches, 80
gin, 128–129, 132–133
gingerbread, 28–29
gold decorating spray, 99
"The Gold-Bug" short story, 52–53, 98, 145

gothic gatherings, 150–152
Gothic Romanticism, 11
Gouda cheese, 26–27, 78–79
grape juice, 140
grapes, 24–25
graveyard cake-decorating sprinkles, 88
Graveyard Poke Cake, 86–88
graveyard-theme cake decorating sprinkles, 40
gummy worms, 108–109

H

ham salad, 16–17
"The Haunted Palace" poem, 80
The Hideous Heart Dessert, 90–91
hideous hints, 152
　black rice, 83
　blood drips, 142–143
　blood spatter, 31, 66–67, 126
　bloody pores, 120
　bloody veins, 76–77
　brainlike appearance, 17
　butter nut squash, 47
　cheese slices, 48
　eyeball garnish, 59
　face of barbarous islander, 71
　gifts for guests, 42
　herbs and flower blossoms, 132–133
　mummy eyes, 27
　pimento-stuffed olives, 53
　potatoes, 37
　skull-shaped pans, 74–75
　spooky faces, 54–55, 63
　stuffed mushroom, 35
　Tombstone Cookies, 114
Hinke, Veronica, 7
House of Usher Party Crackers, 22–23
human heart molds, 90–91
hummus, 21
Hungarian paprika
　Annabel Lee's Crab Bisque, 62–63

Barbarous Islanders' Lobster Newberg, 70–71
Boundaries of Life and Death Party Dip, 16–17
Descent into the Maelstrom Hashed Cod, 81
Patatas Bravas, 36–37
Vulture-Eye Deviled Eggs, 32–33

I

ice cream, 95, 96–97
ice-cube mold, 126
Icy Air of Night Fruit Platter, 30–31
Island of the Fay Rosemary-Scented Baked Stuffed Tomatoes, 57
"The Island of the Fay" short story, 56

K

kale, 78–79
Kirsh liquor, 120–121
kiwi, 30–31

L

Lafourcade Family Graveyard Trifle, 108–109
lavender water, 146
Lemon Compound Butter, 76–77
Lemon Pie, 112
lemon thyme
　House of Usher Party Crackers, 22–23
　Ligeia Dream Cake, 106–107
　The Time Traveler, 126
licorice, 90–91
"The Life and Adventures of Martin Chuzzlewit" (Dickens), 142
life of Edgar Allen Poe, 13
Ligeia Dream Cake, 106–107
"Ligeia" short story, 106–107
literary contributions of Edgar Allan Poe, 13

lobster, 70–71
Loo card game, 158

M

Macko, Stephen, 10
main course, 64–83
　Barbarous Islanders' Lobster Newberg, 70–71
　Catacombs Roasted Cauliflower, 72–73
　Descent into the Maelstrom Hashed Cod, 81
　Ghost Pepper Jelly and Cilantro Cream Cheese Tea Sandwiches, 80
　Prince Prospero's Beef Wellington with Port-Wine Duxelles, 68–69
　Prince Prospero's Roasted Turkey Drumsticks, 66–67
　Raven Black Bean Cakes with Cilantro, 82
　Raven's Nests, 78–79
　Turkey Pudding with Cherry-Cranberry Compote, 74–75
　Vincent Price's Chicken Vermouth with Rice, 83
　Vulture-Eye Pasta, 76–77
mango-pineapple juice, 140
maraschino cherry juice, 30–31
margaritas, 130
marshmallow creme, 30–31
marshmallows, 89
"The Masque of the Red Death" short story, 66, 68–69, 76–77, 92, 120–121
masquerade mask cookie cutter, 69
Mayhew, Henry, 112
meatballs, 58–59
medieval murder-mystery dinner party, 157
Médoc wine, 60–61
melons, 30–31
Meringue Femur Bones, 88
Milk Punch, 147

milk-chocolate bark, 40
Mini Chocolate Skulls, 88, 108–109, 111, 141
mint, 60–61
molasses-poached pears, 114–115
mozzarella, 48, 57
murder-mystery dinner party, 157
"The Murders in the Rue Morgue" short story, 8, 18–20
mushrooms
　Barbarous Islanders' Lobster Newberg, 70–71
　Cadaver Rice, 46–47
　Fortunato's Stuffed Médoc Mushrooms, 35
　Prince Prospero's Beef Wellington with Port-Wine Duxelles, 68–69

N

No-Churn ice cream, 96–97

O

The Oblong Box Cocktail, 128–129
"The Oblong Box" short story, 128–129
olives, 26–27, 53
orange cognac, 144–145
orange liqueur, 140
oranges, 21
oyster crackers, 56

P

pans. See cake pans
paprika. See Hungarian paprika
party planning, 148–159
pasta, 76–77
pastry bites, 38–39
Patatas Bravas, 36–37
peaches, 48, 52–53, 103
pea-flower tea, 124–125
peanuts, 42
pears, 114–115

The Penny Pie Man's Pies, 112
pepper jelly, 80
peppers
 The Assignation Salad, 48
 C. August Dupin's Charcuterie Board, 18–20
 Catacombs Roasted Zucchini and Black Rice with Bell Peppers, 50–51
 Raven's Nests, 78–79
 Shattered Mirror Soup, 58–59
"The Perils of Certain English Prisoners" (Charles Dickens), 132
Philadelphia Fish-House punch, 138–139
pies
 Funeral Pie, 113
 Lemon Pie, 112
 The Penny Pie Man's Pies, 112
 Vinegar Pie, 112
pimento-stuffed olives, 26–27
pistachios, 24–25
Pit and the Pendulum Bread, 28–29
"The Pit and the Pendulum" short story, 28–29, 36–37, 126
The Pit and the Pendulum Spanish Coffee, 126
plums, 48
poblano peppers, 48
Poe, Edgar Allen. See also poetry, by Poe; short stories, by Poe
 diet of, 10
 life of, 13
 literary contributions of, 13
 poetry of, 8
Poe Family Eggnog, 122–123
"The Poe Toaster" ritual, 41, 75
The Poe Toaster's Anchovy Toast Points, 41
poetry, by Poe, 8
 "Annabel Lee," 62–63

"The Bells," 30–31, 124
"The City in the Sea," 94
"Eureka," 140, 146
"Forest Reverie," 24–25
"The Haunted Palace," 80
"To One in Paradise," 114
"The Premature Burial," 17, 38–39, 108–109
"The Raven," 42, 78–79, 82, 104–105
"The Sleeper," 130
"The Thousand-and-Second Tale of Scheherazade," 21
poke cake, 86–88
"Politian" play, 36–37
Poppy-Seed Cake, 106–107
poppy-seed crackers, 22–23
pork, 52–53
port wine, 114–115
port-wine derby, 18–20, 68–69
potatoes
 Arthur Gordon Pym's Clam Chowder, 54–55
 Catacombs Roasted Cauliflower, 72–73
 Descent into the Maelstrom Hashed Cod, 81
 hideous hints for, 37
 Patatas Bravas, 36–37
 Shattered Mirror Soup (Pepper-Pot Soup with Meatballs), 58–59
"The Premature Burial" poem, 17, 38–39, 108–109
Price, Vincent, 83
Prince Prospero's Angel of the Odd Kirsch Mulled Wine with Chokeberries, 120–121
Prince Prospero's Beef Wellington with Port-Wine Duxelles, 68–69
Prince Prospero's Roasted Turkey Drumsticks, 66–67
Prince Prospero's Uninvited Guest Cake, 92–93, 108–109

prosciutto
 C. August Dupin's Charcuterie Board, 18–20
 Prince Prospero's Beef Wellington with Port-Wine Duxelles, 68–69
 Some Words with a Mummy Appetizer, 26–27
pudding
 Turkey Pudding with Cherry-Cranberry Compote, 74–75
 Vanilla Pudding, 108–109, 111
 Vanilla-Perfumed Indian Pudding, 49
puff pastry
 Alarum Premature Burial Fruit-Pastry Bites, 38–39
 Barbarous Islanders' Lobster Newberg, 70–71
 Prince Prospero's Beef Wellington with Port-Wine Duxelles, 68–69
 Some Words with a Mummy Appetizer, 26–27
punch
 Apple Hot Punch, 141
 Descent into the Maelstrom Punch, 138–139
 Eureka Punch, 140
 Milk Punch, 147
 red-berry fruit punch, 138–139
Pym, Arthur Gordon, 40, 54, 70–71

Q

quill cookie cutters, 60–61

R

Randolph, Mary, 34
raspberries
 Alarum Premature Burial Fruit-Pastry Bites, 38–39
 gelatin dessert, 90–91

Raspberry-Rosemary Shrub, 130, 131
 and rosemary shrub margarita, 130
 sauce, 76–77
Raven Black Bean Cakes with Cilantro, 82
"The Raven" poem, 42, 78–79, 82, 104–105
Raven's Nests, 78–79
raven-shaped cookie cutters, 22–23, 104–105
raven-themed snack, 42
Red Death, 120
red-berry fruit punch, 138–139
rice
 Cadaver Rice, 46–47
 Catacombs Roasted Zucchini and Black Rice with Bell Peppers, 50–51
 Vincent Price's Chicken Vermouth with Rice, 83
Roasted Apricots and Bananas Raven Food, 42
Roasted Poblano Pepper Dressing, 48
rosemary
 Island of the Fay Rosemary-Scented Baked Stuffed Tomatoes, 57
 Raspberry-Rosemary Shrub, 131
 The Sleeper, 130
rum, 141

S

salads, 48
salami, 18–20, 26–27
sandwiches, 80
Sangaree, 132–133
sauces, 36–37, 76–77
sausage, 18–20, 26–27
Sazerac cocktail, 126
scallops, 76–77
schnapps, 144–145
Semtner, Christopher P., 10
sesame seeds, black, 22–23
sesame sticks, 42

Shadow Cake, 104–105
Shattered Mirror Soup, 58–59
Sherry Cobbler, 142–143
short stories, by Poe
  "The Angel of the Odd," 103
  "The Assignation," 48, 58–59
  "Berenice," 86, 89
  "The Cask of Amontillado," 35, 50, 60–61, 72, 100–102, 116–117, 122–123
  "A Descent into the Maelstrom," 81, 139
  "Eleanora," 49
  "The Fall of the House of Usher," 22–23, 46–47
  "The Gold-Bug," 52–53, 98, 145
  "The Island of the Fay," 56
  "Ligeia," 106–107
  "The Masque of the Red Death," 66, 68–69, 76–77, 92, 120–121
  "The Murders in the Rue Morgue," 8, 18–20
  "The Oblong Box," 128–129
  "The Pit and the Pendulum," 28–29, 36–37, 126
  "Some Words with a Mummy," 26–27
  "The Tell-Tale Heart," 32–33, 91
sides
  Cadaver Rice, 46–47
  Catacombs Roasted Zucchini and Black Rice with Bell Peppers, 50–51
  Island of the Fay Rosemary-Scented Baked Stuffed Tomatoes, 57
  oyster crackers, 56
  South Carolina Peaches and Pork Tarantula Pull-Apart Bread, 52–53

Vanilla-Perfumed Indian Pudding, 49
Sinbad the Sailor's Roasted Carrot and Blood-Orange Hummus Boats, 21
Sissy's Syllabub, 134–135
skulls
  3D ice-cube mold of, 126
  cake pan of, 30–31, 74–75
  Mini Chocolate Skulls, 88, 108–109, 111, 141
  serving dishes of, 16–17
  shaped candy molds, 111
  shaped jars, 42
The Sleeper (Raspberry-Rosemary Shrub Margarita), 130
"The Sleeper" poem, 130
Some Words with a Mummy Appetizer, 26–27
"Some Words with a Mummy" short story, 26–27
song lists, 159
soup
  Annabel Lee's Crab Bisque, 62–63
  Arthur Gordon Pym's Clam Chowder, 54–55
  Chilled Blackberry Médoc Soup with Fresh Mint, 60–61
  Shattered Mirror Soup, 58–59
South Carolina Peaches and Pork Tarantula Pull-Apart Bread, 52–53
Spanish bun cake, 92–94
Spanish coffee, 126
sprinkles, 40
squid ink, 76–77
squid tentacles, 35
star-shaped aluminum cake pan, 140
strawberries, 38–39
string cheese, 18–20
string licorice, 90–91
stuffed mushrooms, 35
summer sausage, 26–27
Syllabub, 134–135

T
Tavern Biscuits, 34
tea, 124–125
Tea Cakes, 43
tea sandwiches, 80
"The Tell-Tale Heart" short story, 32–33, 91
"The Angel of the Odd" short story, 103
The Assignation Salad, 48
"The Thousand-and-Second Tale of Scheherazade" poem, 21
three-card Loo card game, 158
thyme, 22–23, 126
Tintinnabulation Tea Blend, 124–125
"To One in Paradise" poem, 114
tomatoes, 57
Tombstone Cookies, 88, 89, 108–109, 110
tombstone-shaped cookie cutters, 110
trailed trivia, 154
trifles, 108–109
turkey
  Prince Prospero's Roasted Turkey Drumsticks, 66–67
  Turkey Pudding with Cherry-Cranberry Compote, 74–75

V
vanilla buttercream frosting, 89, 99
Vanilla Pudding, 108–109, 111
Vanilla-Perfumed Indian Pudding, 49
venomous eyes, 28–29
vermouth, 83
Victorian entertaining, 153
Vincent Price's Chicken Vermouth with Rice, 83
Vinegar Pie, 112

violet ice cream, 95
The Virginia Housewife (Mary Randolph), 34
vulture eyes, 18–20
Vulture-Eye Deviled Eggs, 32–33
Vulture-Eye Pasta, 76–77

W
William Legrand's Gold-Bug Cake, 98–99
William Legrand's Gold-Bug Cocktail, 144–145
wine
  Barbarous Islanders' Lobster Newberg, 70–71
  Médoc, 60–61
  port, 114–115
  port-wine derby, 68–69
  Prince Prospero's Angel of the Odd Kirsch Mulled Wine with Chokeberries, 120–121

Z
zucchini, 50–51

ABOUT THE AUTHOR

Veronica Hinke is a culinary and lifestyles journalist and instructor specializing in late nineteenth century and early twentieth century drinking, dining, and entertainment. She is author of *The Last Night on the Titanic: Unsinkable Drinking, Dining & Style*; *Titanic: The Official Cookbook*; *Harry Potter Afternoon Tea Magic*; and *The Great Gatsby Cooking and Entertaining Guide*.

weldon**owen**

an imprint of Insight Editions
P.O. Box 3088
San Rafael, CA 94912
www.weldonowen.com

CEO Raoul Goff
SVP Group Publisher Jeff McLaughlin
VP Publisher Roger Shaw
Publishing Director Katie Killebrew
Executive Editor Edward Ash-Milby
Assistant Editor Kayla Belser
VP, Creative Director Chrissy Kwasnik
Art Director & Designer Megan Sinead Bingham
Production Designer Jean Hwang
Senior Production Manager Joshua Smith
Strategic Production Planner Lina s Palma-Temena

Photography by Stacy Ventura
Food Styling by Victoria Woollard
Food Styling Assistance by Penny Eng

Copyright © 2025 Weldon Owen

All rights reserved. No part of this book may be reproduced in any form without written permission from the publisher.

ISBN: 979-8-88674-231-2

Manufactured in China by Insight Editions
10 9 8 7 6 5 4 3 2 1

Insight Editions, in association with Roots of Peace, will plant two trees for each tree used in the manufacturing of this book. Roots of Peace is an internationally renowned humanitarian organization dedicated to eradicating land mines worldwide and converting war-torn lands into productive farms and wildlife habitats. Roots of Peace will plant two million fruit and nut trees in Afghanistan and provide farmers there with the skills and support necessary for sustainable land use.